Hoofprints

For Setting Up
an Equine-Assisted Therapy Clinic

Naomi Rossthorn
BA, GDPsych, PGPsych, MAPPI.

First published by Busybird Publishing 2021

ISBN
978-1-922691-00-2 (paperback)
978-1-922691-01-9 (ebook)

Cover Image: Grant MacIntyre

Photography: Grant MacIntyre Photography

Cover design: Busybird Publishing

Layout and typesetting: Busybird Publishing

Busybird Publishing
2/118 Para Road
Montmorency, Victoria
Australia 3094
www.busybird.com.au

Hooves represent life for a horse. They enable the horse to move, eat, play, and be part of the herd.

"Since the horse is useful to man only by reason of his movements, his foot deserves the most careful attention. "

Anton Lungwitz
(1897)

The horse symbolises different things to different cultures for some it symbolises mobility, freedom, confidence, nobility, and strength.

Contents

Foreword

Ihave been so very fortunate over the past few months to work closely with Naomi Rossthorn as her business coach and not only have the privilege of getting to know her better, but to also witness her passion for training therapists wishing to incorporate ethical and effective equine-assisted therapy into their practice.

I've also had a front seat as her book, *Hoofprints*, has been brought to life. Lucky me!

I'm a horse lover and rode often as a child. My boys were lucky enough to learn to ride at a much younger age than I did. But the reality is that I'm a city girl and have never had a property suitable for horses of our own. Regardless, the fantasy of 'having a horse' and incorporating it into my work as a psychologist has been in the back of my mind for years. Through talking regularly with Naomi, I have come to understand that there is so much more than just 'having a horse' if you wish to become an equine-assisted therapist. So very much more! Just as there is so much more to becoming a psychologist than 'being a good listener'. Naomi understands the science of psychology and the skill of horsemanship, and how these must intersect if equine-assisted therapy is to be both safe and effective.

If you are hoping to incorporate horses into your work as a therapist, I highly recommend you start with shifting your thinking beyond 'having a horse' and onto absorbing the knowledge and skill that Naomi brings to her books and training programs.

Hoofprints brings Naomi's life experiences, training, and professional skill to the fore, wrapped up in her passion for safe and effective equine-assisted therapy. I know you'll love this book!

Dr Tess Crawley
Psychologist & Business Coach

It is my great privilege to introduce you to Naomi Rossthorn, fellow psychologist, Founder of Harnessing Wellness Psychology in the beautiful Yarra Ranges and passionate Thought Leader in the field of Equine-assisted Psychological Interventions.

You just need to spend five minutes with Naomi to realise that she has an uncanny ability to harness the powerful human-equine bond towards healing emotional wounds whilst rebuilding worth, confidence and meaning in the people she supports.

Naomi has spent many years perfecting the strategies and interventions critical to harnessing wellness for her human clients through their interactions with their equine partners in therapy. As such, she is able to offer a highly ethical, professional, client-focused, best practice model of equine-assisted psychology.

In *Hoofprints*, Naomi outlines a number of scientist practitioner case studies, which lifts the veil on the how-to of running equine-assisted therapeutic interventions in private practice and other similar settings.

If you are interested in introducing equine-assisted psychology into your clinical work, then you have found the right book. Naomi takes you through the how-to of introducing this powerful service offering into your practice from a practical standpoint, whilst addressing the underlying theoretical framework which defines equine-assisted psychology.

As a psychologist first and foremost, Naomi is acutely aware of the ethics behind ensuring an evidence-based approach to implementing equine-assisted psychology as part of mainstream psychological interventions.

As a private practice owner myself, I fully appreciate the unique service offering created by providing equine-assisted psychology. Naomi has skilfully acknowledged this, whilst encapsulating it within the evidence base of practical psychology principles and a high level of customer service and client-informed treatment.

I highly recommend this book to any health professional who is interested to learn more about Equine-assisted Psychology and its application within the mental health, allied health, and general health field.

Hoofprints will give you the theory as well as the practicalities of what has to be considered. Coupled with the passion that Naomi has for this field, it makes for a great read.

Gerda Muller
Clinical Psychologist | Published Author
Private Practice Success Business Coach & Mentor

About Naomi Rossthorn

Naomi Rossthorn, a registered psychologist, has been partnering with horses for human wellness since 2010. Here is the hoofprints version for incorporating horses into your psychology or therapy practice and partnering with therapy horses for human wellness.

In 2010, Naomi developed an adjunct trauma-sensitive Experiential Horse Therapy Program for those affected by Black Saturday Bushfires and delivered the program to children, adolescents and adults. Since 2010, she has developed and co-facilitated Equine-assisted Therapy and Psychology programs for children and adolescents exposed to complex family environments, as well as trauma-sensitive programs for children, adolescents and adults affected by natural disasters, including bushfire-affected communities and, more recently, the COVID-19 pandemic.

Naomi was trained in the science practitioner model and has over the years collected the Equine-assisted Psychology (EAP) program data to explore and report the data related to the efficacy of EAP programs. She continues to work as a psychologist and with horses for human wellness.

Dedication

Thank you to the amazing people who love horses, who I have met along this journey, and who have taught me so much.

To those who are devoted to advocating, educating and finding a better way to understand and treat equines in the world today. I want to specifically thank Dr Christine Gee, Andrew Bowe, and Dr Paul Owen: through our conversations, you have deepened my understanding of equines and their psychology and physical attributes and taught me to value the equine as a sentient being. Through your extended knowledge to pursue best practice for caring, training and treating many equines in a holistic way, the herd and I will be forever grateful for meeting you.

Dedicated to Trigger, Kankukadale Golden Ticket: you were my compass to learn all things horse. May your soul rest in peace knowing you helped so many. You were my much-loved therapy horse and for that I thank you dearly.

Hoofprints

W elcome to *Hoofprints for Setting Up an Equine-Assisted Therapy Clinic*. You are reading this because you are either interested in learning more about equine-assisted therapy or because you are considering adding this adjunct therapy into your psychology or therapy practice.

The motivation behind putting this book together is educational: to present an informed holistic way to incorporate horses into therapy exploring psychological, physical and environmental factors to support mental health professionals, the horses in therapy and the clients and participants.

Since 2003, my research and training has included learning the how-to for incorporating horses and ponies into psychology and counselling. This is a compilation, a guidebook of my personal and professional learning, my hoofprints of implementing equine-assisted therapy successfully into my private psychology practice.

Disclaimer: This book is written with the information based on Victorian and Australian equine guidelines and safety information. Please refer to your state or country's equine welfare and safety legislation, acts and guidelines for most relevant information to your horse care and for your equine-assisted therapy practice protocols. Throughout this book I refer to equine as horses and ponies (collectively) and sometimes I write 'horses' which also includes ponies for the sake of brevity. I do not include information specifically on zebras, donkeys or mules as I am not familiar with them, however, they are part of the equine genesis.

IMPORTANT WARNING: about working with and participating in activities with horses:

Equine-assisted psychology/therapy activities can be highly active and participation in such warrants caution. Improper use of information described in this written material and any online training and misapplication to a social learning or treatment program may result in serious injury and/or death. Neither the author Naomi Rossthorn nor any other contributor assume any liability for loss or damage, direct or consequential to readers, participants, or others from the use of this proposed material. Case study details were changed for privacy and confidentiality and any likeness is purely coincidence. Permission was given verbally and in writing by the clients (or their parents and/or guardians if they were underage) for images to be used for educational purposes only and they are not to be copied. All of the information in this book is copyrighted.

Step One

The First Step

*I think sometimes we need to take a step back and
just remember we have no greater right to be here
than any other animal.*

– David Attenborough

When I was 17 years old, during the summer of 1994–1995, I was on a student exchange in Nagoya, Japan. On the evening of 16 January 1995, following two days of wandering around Kobe exploring ancient temples with my host family, we returned to Nagoya before school was to start the following day.

On 17 January 1995 at 5.46 am in the southern part of Hyōgo Prefecture there was an earthquake, later called the Kobe earthquake or the Great Hanshin. We felt the earthquake in Nagoya at my host family's house. I was not sure what was going on but the whole house moved. My host father appeared standing in the bedroom doorway I shared with my host sister, as the house swayed. He was telling us to do something, which I could not understand as my shock and stress levels were high. I copied my host sister and quickly got dressed for school and went to the kitchen. The aftershocks continued and we were to stay under the kitchen table eating our breakfast before we left for school.

I was grateful to connect with my school friends who spoke English so we could discuss what was happening. We had a calligraphy class with Mr Shodo (Shodö means calligraphy in Japanese), who was reassuring and explained in broken English what had happened and gave our class a 'What to do in an earthquake and aftershock speech'. There were predications by some of my classmates who were listening to their 'elders' that the next earthquake was to be closer to Nagoya. I became fearful for my life and worried I would not be able to return home. I had two weeks left before I was to return to Australia to start Year 12, my final year at high school.

Due to disaster management, telephone lines and resources were redirected and I was unable to get hold of my family in Australia. Eventually I did but it was after a few days. They had been trying to reach me too, having known we were travelling to Kobe and were not sure if all was well with me. I begged them to book a flight to get home sooner, but there were no flights leaving or arriving at that time. I had to endure a very long two weeks. When I finally get on the flight to go home to Melbourne, as the flight was circling the Melbourne airport, I sobbed with relief and happiness to be home.

Sadly, 6,434 people lost their lives and about 4,600 of them were in Kobe. Japanese disaster prevention authorities began installing rubber blocks under bridges and spacing buildings further apart to try to reduce damage in the future. This was a narrow escape for my host family and for weeks after the earthquake, watching the television and hearing through school friends, I learnt of the devastation that the earthquake caused on a massive scale.

This event changed me. It opened my eyes. It sparked my curiosity about natural disasters, survivor guilt, resilience, and recovery. This experience had nothing to do with horses at the time. However, 15 years later, in 2009, I found myself working in another natural disaster – The Black Saturday bushfires in Victoria, Australia, a devastating bushfire in which 173 people lost their lives, left many people homeless, and caused a massive loss of livestock, fauna and flora.

It was following this bushfire that I began working with horses in equine-assisted therapy. However, horses became part of my life in my early twenties. I started horse riding following a relationship breakdown. Before this relationship ended, I enjoyed going out and was a social person, but we had a mutual friendship group which made socialising after the breakup difficult.

At the time I was living by myself, worked fulltime, and decided to fill in time by pursuing further studies in psychology. I was curious about relationships, grief, coping strategies and building resilience, having grown up with loving grandparents who were prisoners of war in WWII. On weekends, I left the city and went trail riding through the hills with groups of random people who signed up and paid to ride trail horses for three hours. I loved it! I did this for months – it was my distraction and it gave me freedom.

I rode different horses each week and as my ability to stay on improved, I was allocated horses who were rated as more difficult. There was no technique to my riding and no relationship with the horse, but my aim was not to fall off.

Travelling overseas became another distraction, with equines remaining to be part of these trips. I had been able to stay on bolting horses in New Zealand, donkeys while travelling through Egypt, all the while ducking tree branches and running up and down hills – with sheer luck, I suspect.

Country life was a thought but never a reality for me. I loved comedy and Billy Crystal was a favourite comedian of mine. I enjoyed the movie *City Slickers* – a cowboy comedy about a cattle

muster, relationships and finding a spark in life – and the thought of driving cattle had a certain appeal. Curly said, 'There's nothing like bringing in a herd.' *Great*, I thought, *Where can I do that?* I spoke to my cousin and told him I wanted to do a cattle muster. He laughed but agreed, so I found an 11-day course on how to be a Jackaroo/Jillaroo.

We drove 10 or so hours interstate and arrived at a working farm/station. I did not really know what that meant, but I knew I was going to learn to muster cattle.

We arrived at the old homestead and it was beautiful, with a wrap-around veranda and climbing roses. The females slept in bunkrooms in the house and the males were in the shearing shed. Breakfast was served with the hot milk straight from the cow which we all took turns in milking minutes before (sorry that still makes me gag).

There were about 15 people who attended, made up of mostly European backpackers, but there were also a couple of young local boys – on 'probation' who were sent to learn basic farmhand skills – and my cousin and I, the city slickers.

I quickly learnt that real cowboys got on with the job: a broken nail meant your nails were too long, crying meant dust was in your eyes and complaining meant the job took longer because you were wasting time. I learnt that helplessness was laughed at and if you did not get your chores done, you were yelled at – hello backbone, I think you are growing!

I had never saddled a horse before, but my cousin had – he got in trouble for helping me so I had to learn to do it myself. I learnt that you had no time for worry and if the saddle was not put on your horse properly, and in my case I slid off a few times, you had to stop, get off the horse or fix it, and then gallop after the others to catch up. I was called by my surname and my name became Ross from the first day on. Not sure if you would call it tough love or tough work.

The day came and we were going to bring in a herd. We left early morning after breakfast, I just had toast, and we were told we were moving cattle and sheep from one paddock to another. The horse I was on knew I was a phony and could not ride well and within 10 minutes she bolted down a hill. The cowboy must have thought that was dangerous and made Ellen, a nice Dutch girl, get off her horse and swap with me. Jewel (in the photo left) was my second horse on the journey and we were going to bring in the herd.

At last we were droving cattle! I was in heaven sitting on my new 'safe' horse watching the cows move in front. I learnt that you never try to separate a mother cow from her calf because she would protect it, and I was not keen to know what she did to protect her calf. So now I was a cowgirl, a city slicker jillaroo, bringing in the herd.

I was so pleased with myself and I was enjoying the meander and daydreaming, when I watched a calf break away from the herd and run down the hill next to me. Like a lightning bolt I was struck out of my lovely moment and I heard 'Ross, get the bloody thing!' Adrenaline flooded my nervous system, my eyes widened and I had to get the 'bloody thing'! The cowboy was yelling at me, so with a hand on the reins, my heartbeat thumping loudly in my ears, I turned and looked at the calf and kicked my horse Jewel.

The right side of my brain was crying and kept telling me we were going to die. My left side of my brain was logical, practical and focused. We went left down the hill, the calf went right. I stared at the calf like my life depended on it – well, I think it probably did with the cowboy watching. Jewel went right, then the calf went left and Jewel went left. I thought, *Let's go on the outside of the calf to push it back toward the herd*, and Jewel and I moved to the outside of the calf and manoeuvred it back into the herd. I did not feel connected to my body at that time, I felt a rush of excitement and bewilderment and I did it. When the rush wore off, I knew I did not have the skill to move a horse like that so she must have been trained and knew what to do, or maybe she read my mind? I felt so much relief – I did not die and I got a 'Good job, Ross!' YES!!

I realised that for some reason Jewel had done what I wanted. The idea that thoughts and body movement could move a horse 'without just staying on' made me curious to find out what had happened. Could it happen again?

Convinced Jewel knew what I wanted her to do, I began reading, researching horses and communication and the connection between humans and horses. 'Can horses read minds?' 'How do horses learn to catch cows?' 'Can horses communicate telepathically?' Ridiculous questions. I then came across *The Tao of Equus* by Linda Kohanov, a book about Linda's journey of healing and transformation through the way of the horse. Then I found Klaus Hempfling's book *Dancing with Horses*, in which he describes *equilibrio natural* – natural balance, 'a process of communication between two beings by the subtlest, almost invisible signals, through pure thought and feeling'. This was it. I was not mad, others had experienced it too! The human-horse connection was a new fascination and became a passion for me and complemented my interest in human psychology.

Fast forward to now, following my years of study, training and learning, I believe that my professional identity is firstly as a registered psychologist, as it is a regulated profession, and secondly in my work with horses in adjunct equine-assisted therapy. At this stage in Australia, being an equine-assisted therapist is not a regulated profession and there appears to be limited, rigorous replicated clinical research supporting equine-assisted therapy as an evidenced-based practice. The field of animal-assisted therapy is in its infancy in terms of specific data / research to show change, but it is a growing field and will continue to be supported by more rigorous replicated research.

A mission of mine was to try to turn my anecdotal theory of improved wellbeing of client case studies when interacting with horses into a research-based and evidence-based practice, with the hope that it would begin to set a best practice standard for other psychologists and mental health professionals. But this takes time and resources, hence my writing of this book.

I do believe equine-assisted therapy is a valuable form of adjunct animal-assisted therapy for some clients, so much so that I have added it to my psychology clinic to assist people in harnessing wellness. Trigger, Happy, Bob and Bailey are the equine partners who work in the clinic.

Trigger (Kanikadale Golden Ticket), 10-year-old Holsteiner x Sporthorse gelding, was bred for competition but was not able to meet the demands due to his sway back.

Happy, a 25-year-old Australian riding pony in retirement from being a children's pony.

Bob, rising five, named after Bob Marley due to a mane that becomes dreadlock-like in winter. Do not be deceived by his cuteness. He is a registered miniature horse but looks more like a Shetland pony.

This is Bailey, who is generally with Bob. He is 10 years old. He is a Shetland pony. He has a beautiful nature. He lives next door and comes through the fence to visit daily. He would volunteer to participate with Bob in equine-assisted therapy sessions so he became part of the team.

Step Two

Safe Connections

*Being able to feel safe with others is probably the
single most important aspect of mental health.
Safe connections are fundamental to meaningful
and satisfying lives.*

– Bessel Van Der Kolk

Trigger, the Dangerous Horse

As with humans all horses have an instinctual need to feel safe. All horses can be dangerous, their instincts can override previous training, and they move quickly to keep themselves safe. Before Trigger, a rising four-year-old 16.6 hands, Warmblood Palomino, came into my life, I had not given too much thought about how dangerous horses could be. I was advised that Trigger was easy to handle, trim and worm. It was a farrier who called him dangerous – Trigger reared up as she tried to lift his feet. He was so tall standing on his hindquarters. She packed up her tools and told me he needed more training and was dangerous. I had never seen Trigger behave like that with anyone before. No one was injured but I had a new understanding of how Trigger, who was going to be a therapy horse, had the potential to be a danger to someone.

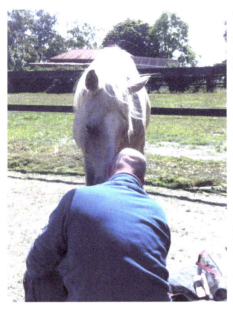

The photo to the 'left' was the first one I took of trigger. It was the day he had arrived to the agistment venue, after five days travelling by truck from Queensland to Victoria. Trigger looked exhausted, thin and I guess wanting to connect. This photo was a perfect example of his nature. He walked up to my husband who had strained his back from lifting at work and stood with him forehead to forehead. For Trigger, the move from Queensland, where he had lived in a paddock with one other horse, to the agistment place in Victoria where he shared a large paddock with 15 horses at any one time, was a big one. The paddock herd was reasonably transient, many horses would come and go from the paddock. About five horses had been there consistently for years.

I was two months pregnant with my second child when Trigger was kindly gifted to me by a friend and colleague who was moving overseas. Trigger had a sway back and mild scoliosis and although he was beautiful, he was not going to be able to meet the ongoing training demands as a dressage horse due to his conformation. I had nothing in the way of horse gear. I had to buy him a halter, lead rope, brushes, rugs, feed buckets, and food.

Every two days I would drive an hour and a half to visit Trigger. It was too far to carry the food to his paddock, so I would walk to the big paddock to find him. I would stand in the paddock and call him, then stick my arm up in the air and wait. Sometimes, the horses would run as a herd, the thunder of their hooves overwhelming as they all came towards me and I would get out of the way. Sometimes, Trigger would wander out from behind some trees and come to me. I would halter him and walk from the big paddock up a hill through two gates to some stables, where I would sit on a milk crate next to him and give him a biscuit of lucerne and some vitamin pellets. I loved listening to him eat. Then I would brush him and walk him back to the paddock. In winter, the nights were cold, sometimes around zero. I often checked the temperature and worried if Trigger would be cold or hungry. I felt I needed to know more about equine husbandry and first aid.

It appeared that Trigger was bitten by other horses, with new flesh wounds appearing. I would dress the wounds with antiseptic. Trigger had seedy toe, which was re-occurring, that I would plug with Vaseline and copper sulphate. Trigger developed mud fever around his pasterns and coronets, so I had to learn how to treat his heels using Sudocrem as a barrier to moisture. Towards the end of the first year, Trigger had warts on his muzzle, apparently this was not uncommon for young horses. His friend, Rex, a beautiful Clydesdale the same age as Trigger also developed warts over his muzzle, much to the dismay of Rex's owner and myself. They both recovered. The fact that they had shared it with each other meant the two were playing together. This gave me comfort that he had a friend.

The agistment place was busy and I had some interesting interactions with other agistees. A young woman made a comment about the differences between our two horses. When she would walk her horse back to the paddock, as soon as she

took the halter off her horse, he would gallop (almost fly) back to the herd. I would have the opposite issue: I had to pull on Trigger's halter to try to get him to walk back into the paddock through the gate. He would plant his front feet and would stand still and would not want to go back in. The comment the

woman made was that she wished her horse would like to spend time with her like Trigger appeared to want to stay with me. I think that Trigger liked the attention, the brush and the food, and it was a pleasant association with me.

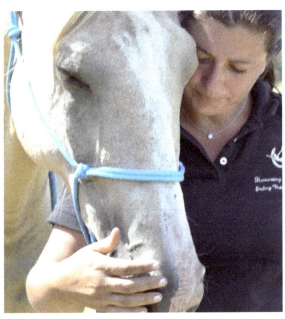

Nothing happens in isolation of other factors, it never does. There is always a context. So here is the context of that incident with the farrier that called Trigger a dangerous horse. She arrived, she was running late, she did not regard Trigger or say hello to him; she just wanted to do her job and quickly, fair enough. Trigger was sniffing her hair as she was leaning over to pick up his front hoof. I was holding his lead rope. He sniffed my hair all the time, I never thought  anything of it. The farrier grabbed the rope off of me and backed him up hard, turned him around quickly. She was hard on his head, and it took both of us by surprise. I think Trigger reared in fear and he did not understand what she was asking of him. Then she commented, 'He's a dangerous horse, he needs to be worked and trained and I am not going to trim his feet.' She packed up and left. I was stunned and sat down. I felt sick and had a terrible feeling in my stomach. What have I done taking on this horse? He was going to be a therapy horse but he will not lift his feet and now he will not get trimmed because he is dangerous. Those words echoed in my ears, *Trigger is a dangerous horse*. I did not fear Trigger, but I now worried I did not know enough about how to train and care for horses.

I had a conundrum: I was four months pregnant and I had a dangerous horse that I was supposed to work with in therapy with people; but I never moved on my animals once they were part of my family. So I made a choice: I chose to learn and work on how to work with Trigger to support him as a great therapy horse. I had to work out what I needed to do to make myself a good enough horse person.

I started watching, reading and learning *different horse training methods and philosophies* because I knew that I needed more skills on the ground. I watched other people at the agistment property and how they treated their horses.

I saw people treat their horses aggressively and the names they called their horses were terrible. They appeared not to watch their horse's body language or reactions. There was no relationship. If I was their horse, I would gallop away from them as fast as I could too. I remember a young woman dressed up in a beautiful dressage outfit. Her horse looked lovely with a beautiful saddle, matching halter and leg wraps. Once he was tacked up, she mounted him outside the agistment gate, but he would not walk forward and she began whipping him. There was hard rubbish waiting to be collected at the front gate. The horse appeared to be unsure of the hard rubbish pile and did not want to walk past it. This young lady whipped her horse so hard I could hear it. She also swore at him. I was shocked and asked if she would like me to help her and offered the suggestion that maybe he was scared of the rubbish pile. She yelled at me that it was ridiculous and that he should not be scared of rubbish.

Well, as a prey animal, how does he know the rubbish would not eat him? She hit him hard with her whip – over and over. It did not look nice at all. I decided that I was not going to do that and I was disturbed that she thought whipping was a good way to make her horse walk. But what would I know? I had a dangerous horse!

It was this lady, who whipped her horse, that had commented that my horse appeared to like me, as Trigger and I sat in the sun, and that she wished her horse wanted to spend time with her.

At the time I smiled and did not say anything. Since the incident with the abrasive farrier, I have been the bystander a few times to people handling Trigger in a way I did not agree with. I assumed the 'horse person' knew more than me and I allowed them to handle him roughly. I now choose people carefully and let them know how to handle my horses and ponies before they do. I am my horses and ponies advocate in that area. This continues to happen during equine-assisted therapy sessions and I will talk more about how I do that in later chapters.

After a year and a half, I was kindly offered a paddock next to the property that I was going to work from and I took it. I booked a truck to take Trigger to the other property. When the truck arrived, I was nervous and my voice was not working well. I had to get Trigger, the dangerous horse, onto the truck. The truck driver was one of the most sensible people I had met on the journey thus far. He said, 'Let's just go slowly, I find these jobs happen quicker the slower we take it.'

So I walked Trigger onto the truck and he followed me trustingly. The man locked him into the truck and Trigger started calling. He did not know where he was going and he did not know he was never going to see his friend Rex again. I drove behind the truck until we arrived at the new home which was 30 minutes away.

When he got out of the truck, we lead him into the paddock and he ran around with some new horses: an older horse named Milo, a Shetland pony called Peppy – who became attached to Trigger – and a little Shetland pony named Bailey (later to work in therapy sessions with us). I engaged a horse trainer with a holistic horsemanship approach and a new farrier to work with. Both were gentle but firm, understood horses from a horse's perspective and I felt I had a team and some support. Trigger responded well to both of them. I am grateful to them.

Following the arrival of my second child, I did not ride Trigger. I learnt to work with him on the ground. The importance of training and working with him made me realise that the relationship we had was important. It made me realise that I wanted to work with him, not just any horse. I knew his strengths and challenges and still now, I know Trigger watches me in therapy sessions to take cues. I have had to work a lot on myself to become aware of my shortcomings and build my confidence as a horse person. I have learnt many strategies including picking up feet and being able to shift Trigger out of his right (rioting) side of his brain and into the left (thinking) side of his brain. I have also learnt to assess how he behaves and psychologically, to see whether or not he's ready to work and to be around people.

My learning curve while being with Trigger has certainly been a big one. I once heard someone say that you will get a horse to teach you and then a horse to reward you. Trigger taught me what I needed to learn about horses, and I began to understand them as feeling, thinking and social mammals with the amazing ability to attune and to attach to others for their survival.

As a psychologist, when a client comes to talk with me: I listen, I observe and I try to understand using a therapeutic framework. Horse handling is very much about looking at, listening to and understanding the horse. It is more than moving a horse; handling is about feel. It is understanding the history of the horse, the context and the welfare of the horse from the horse's perspective as much as possible. Research published by Rachele Malavasi and Ludwig Huber (2016) infers that horses can not only read humans but can adopt behaviours to try to communicate with them.[1]

It is called Heterospecific Referential Communication, which describes a process of using a gesture; like eye contact, a horse pushing a gate with their heads, or using their mouth to show you where they would like a scratch. Their gesture is to direct the attention of the person to get their desired goal; for example, a scratch. It was also found that horses increased their communication by changing from a visual cue to a tactile one and they demonstrated persistence in their communication

---

1. Malavasi R, Huber L. 'Evidence of heterospecific referential communication from domestic horses (*Equus caballus*) to humans.' *Anim Cogn.* 2016 Sep;19(5):899-909. DOI: 10.1007/s10071-016-0987-0. Epub 2016 Apr 20. PMID: 27098164.

gesture. This is really important in equine-assisted therapy sessions, to be observant of your horse's communication. If you are observant, then you can work out what a horse is communicating, like pushing at a gate to get out of the work area and also what their interaction is like with the client. This insight into horses adds value to better understanding horse psychology and behaviour.

We would not use an intervention for mental health unless we trained and understood it, so why would we include horses in therapy if we did not understand them well on the ground, or understand their needs and wants, and factor that support in to make them feel safe? Therapeutic rapport is an essential part of therapy. The aim is to model good, healthy relationships so the client feels safe and respected. It is the same with horses. Their safety means survival.

Prior to Trigger coming into my life, I worked with different horses and ponies in equine-assisted therapy. I contracted people to assist with the horse handling and these horses were generally owned by those people. The ponies and horses had their own history, possibly multiple owners and training in disciplines such as dressage and show jumping. These horses all had their own characters, but in the equine-assisted therapy sessions my focus was on the clients and the activities, rather than getting to know the horses individually.

Having worked with Trigger, Happy, Bailey and Bob on a regular basis, I believe that the expectations, stress and pressure of a therapy horse is different than on a horse that is to be ridden, though it is no less important. Therefore, the treatment, handling and therapeutic activities required within equine-assisted psychology sessions does require that the therapy horse has a different type of training and understanding of their work. The expectations in therapy sessions require a robust connection between the horse and the therapeutic facilitator to support them, and they in turn need an understanding of equine behaviour. Horses do what makes sense to them. They will do their best to look after themselves moment to moment. All horses can be dangerous when they do not understand what is being asked of them or perceive an action as aggressive or threatening towards them. That is why I believe learning horse psychology and behaviour is so important for horses, facilitators and participants of equine-assisted therapy.

Step Three

Understanding Horses

Mindful thought is the minute-by-minute awareness of everything that is going on in and around you.

– Unknown

The horse and pony are not mythical beings, nor are they the therapists.

The quote above on mindfulness describes how horses live. This chapter covers basic areas of equine physiology, psychology and behaviour that enhance the mental health professionals' work with equines. I encourage you to have a keen interest in all things horses and to learn as much as you can about this species if you choose to work with them.

Further study and learning about horse's physiology and psychology has been to better my practice with horses and what I can offer my clients in sessions. I find that I can only offer in horse knowledge and handling what I know and understand, and I can only draw on my knowledge of horses in terms of metaphor for client self-care. For example: by discussing with a client how a horse's need for self-care is their survival and how it overrides them taking risks may be a way to introduce topics such as risk-taking behaviour. Furthermore, I can only care for my horses at the level I understand. I aim to learn and be the best horse person I can be, and I encourage you to be the best you can be for them too.

Horses are prey mammals

Horses are prey mammals and their instincts and nervous system are wired to live in the present moment to assess and receive information from the environment to sense danger cues. As prey mammals, their brains are wired to search (and not hunt) for grass, leaves, water, shelter, herds mates and be hypervigilant to danger. Movement is their life and another key to their survival. Horses can stand within an hour after birth. They use their legs to survive by running, kicking, rearing and bucking. They can be quiet and walk up behind you without a sound. Their inherent instinct for 'flight before thought mode' means they can sense and outrun their predators. Therefore, horses will often run from a perceived threat first, then question the object or the thing they are running from second. This will be done by turning and facing the threat. This is useful to understand when training a therapy horse, and in terms of adopting relaxation-first training practices. I will go into more horse training ideas in chapter nine.

Horses attune to their herd members for survival. In the mammalian brain, the limbic system resonates and horses' nervous systems attune (same with humans), facilitating an energetic nervous system vibration and connection, to allow horses to sense if there is a threat and respond as a herd. They are hardwired to do this. This survival instinct has meant that they focus and value relationships and a hierarchy system with other mammals, preferably equines, over the territory they live in. There is safety in numbers.

In equine-assisted therapy sessions, working with small herds can be helpful to support the equines, as they have each other. Even if I have one horse in the arena, the venue we work from is set up so the other herd members are in view and can touch each other over the arena fence.

I have heard horse trainers say, 'Horses are anxiety on four legs.' This is because they live in their sympathetic nervous system. Sometimes, I introduce the therapy horses in this way at the start of a session, depending on the issue of the client and where appropriate. Some clients have commented, 'I can relate to that.' It has become a useful phrase for trying to build rapport with some clients and begin discussions around mental health symptoms as part of the psycho-education component of therapy.

Horses are relational

Equines are relational mammals; they have authentic relationship interactions in which they do not bribe or manipulate for their individual benefit. Their herd hierarchy is based on clear verbal and non-verbal communication with other herd members. Horses naturally live in herds for socialisation and protection.

The more horses, the more eyes, ears and senses there are on the lookout for danger. There are also more options for the predator to choose from, reducing the risk of it being them.

They generally pair bond with another within the herd, with a horse friend who may be the same or similar colour or be around the same age if given the right environment and enough herd members. The 'like likes like' formula applies here.

In equine-assisted therapy sessions, horses provide interactions for people to feel connection with another in a non-judgmental fashion. Like Trigger smelling my hair when I fed him, it is the feeling of the warmth of his nose, the gentle touch and moments of companionship that can change a person's experience of feeling alone in that moment. With permission, I take photos of moments of connection during the session, to give the client to take home. I have designed a Harnessing Wellness Horse Therapy Journal for this purpose. This aids in evoking a visual memory of the moment; through neuroplasticity it can support a client create a new memory of connection, aiding a client to reflect on their session between visits.

Horses play to offset prey instinct

Horses' ability to socialise and live in herds enables them to be curious and playful, and they enjoy playing as it breaks the stress of being a prey animal. This can be done in a few ways: they can push chairs over in a therapy session, chew people's hats, wiggle lead ropes, pick up cones, and move balls, etc. They can also nibble each other on the back of their legs and mouth each other on their lips. They can also use their back side to bang into other horses and they might start doing it to you if they think you are an equal, a playmate like another horse, and while it can be entertaining for the horse, it is not always entertaining in therapy sessions.

Understanding the difference between your therapy horse playing and asserting themselves in the herd (including with you) is important to know what to do next. I do not encourage therapy equine's mouthing people; if they seek that contact with their muzzle, then I rub their noses with my hand and apply a little pressure and they usually move their heads away. I am then not too much fun to play with but not disrespectful. It was during a group therapy session that someone I hired to assist me with the horses, hit Bob, the pony on his muzzle, to teach him a lesson. I could not believe it. Being aware of horse behaviour gives you choice for the interaction. If the horse or pony was encroaching on my space, I can choose to ask them to back up with or without touch to reiterate where I am in the

hierarchy. Horses and ponies that yield to gentle pressure are ideal in these scenarios. Trigger is beautiful at moving backwards, I can look at him and point over his shoulder and use that hand in a motion and he will step back.

Trigger also loves shoes. He will bite my shoes, and I know he is playing but it's not ideal for him to see me as a play friend.

In this photo Trigger is biting my foot. Trigger is very playful and while I know he is playing, I would not allow him to do this with clients.

Here is when I usually ask him to take a few steps back to assert herd dominance. Although I do find it funny, (refer to photo on previous page) I do not know what exactly I was doing, but here is Trigger biting my shoe.

Horses who live and work with humans require the human to teach the horse what to do in a human world. Horses do what makes sense to them and humans give labels to their behaviours. Therefore, when working with horses we need to 'think more like a horse'. We should take time to teach those interacting with horses, especially people new to interacting with horses, how to read a horse's body language. At the time of writing this book, one person a day is hospitalised in Australia for a horse-related injury. For more information please refer to safeworkaustralia.gov.au and the guidelines for working with those new to horses.

It is a duty of care to look after our clients when around our therapy horses and ponies. There will be more about professional

responsibility and legislation in chapter five. However, taking time to watch the therapy horses and ponies is another way to extend observational skills, learn non-verbal herd language, as well as to learn and build on attention and mindfulness skills. It also gives client's choices in therapy sessions for self-care. For example: if they feel a horse is too close and they feel unsafe, they can move away. It also personalises a horse from an object to a living, breathing, sentient being, to focus on horse welfare, which I feel is so important.

Humans are predators

Humans are considered predators to horses. We have our eyes on the front of our head and claws (hands with nails), not hooves. We can eat meat if we choose, and our instincts were designed to hunt and gather. Humans are goal-oriented, we have both predator and prey instincts (fight and flight) and therefore we walk towards and can 'go after' the horse. Even though horses are domesticated and can be trained to be around people, the predator-prey dynamic is part of the human-horse evolution. Therefore, horses and ponies in a therapy session, can wonder if we are going to harm or to eat them, or if we are safe. If we act like a predator in an equine-assisted therapy session (walk up quickly to the horse, jump at them), the horse can respond by fleeing from us by emotionally shutting down, physically running away, or disengage from the equine therapy session. I have seen it where a horse's eyes will glaze over, they shut down emotionally due to their previous training in which they have learnt to tolerate what was being done to them. Happy used to do it. He would stand still, his lips purse, and tense in anticipation. I leave Happy untethered when meeting new people, it gives him choice to move away. In some sessions, Happy will seek contact and he loves a scratch and brush on his terms and in other sessions he will not engage.

In a therapy session, psychologists and mental health practitioners need to work on their own emotions to form a sense of congruency in their body, by becoming present and slowing their breathing, for the horse to feel safe. If we are heightened in energy, the horse can attune and can also become heightened. Horses attune to our limbic and nervous system, which is what makes them wonderful to work with.

Toileting behaviour and relaxation

Horses generally urinate when they feel safe and they do so approximately five times a day. Horses can run and defecate at the same time and can defecate up to 15 kilograms of manure a day, so this is not a behaviour they use to show relaxation. Sometimes I talk about this, depending on the context and therapeutic goal, and when the horse or pony urinate some people talk about the horse feeling more relaxed.

Healthy manure should fall into lumps and break as it hits the ground, I check my horses' poo and watch them urinate regularly as this gives me basic information on their health. Sloppy poo could mean too much grass or an tummy upset. Cloudy wee needs to be monitored for potential dehydration or kidney issues. Always check with your vet if you have concerns.

Hooves and health

Horses are designed to move and run. On an average day, wild horses in outback Australia travel up to 15 kilometres. Some were recorded walking up to 55 km from their watering points, and some horses walked for 12 hours to water from feeding grounds.[2]

Horses have evolved from a four-toed, dog-like animal into the single-toed mammal. The hoof is made up of several different layers and structures, each with a specific function. The functions of the hoof are to feel the ground (proprioception), enable rest, as well as help with blood circulation. Healthy hooves, healthy horse.

Movement not only supports horses (and humans) to manage their nervous system and energy, it enables the horse's hooves, which are essentially suspension pads, to pump fresh blood up their leg from the base of the hoof. This moves blood and oxygen around the horse. The hooves also cushion the impact of the legs on the ground. Without movement, horses can develop various health issues.

Research has shown that less movement and isolation for horses has been linked with reduced wellbeing, heightened stress and depression.[3] Domesticated horses differ in their behavioural and physiological responses to isolated and group housing. At the venue I work from, we built a track system. The pasture was divided up using hot tape and temporary fencing, into a figure-eight shape to keep the horses moving.

My herd's farrier, the Barehoof Blacksmith, often looks at the outside of the hooves for surface rings, changes in colour

2. Hampson BA, de Laat MA, Mills PC, Pollitt CC. 'Distances travelled by feral horses in "outback" Australia.' *Equine Vet J Suppl.* 2010 Nov;(38):582-6. DOI: 10.1111/j.2042-3306.2010.00203.x PMID: 21059064

3. Hall C, Royle C, Walker SL, Yarnell K. 'Domesticated horses differ in their behavioural and physiological responses to isolated and group housing.' *Physiology & Behaviour.* 2015 May; 143: 51-57. https://doi.org/10.1016/j.physbeh.2015.02.040

and texture, which we discuss. The condition of the hooves is represented by undulated surface rings that tell the history of the horse's stress, dietary issues, health, bouts of laminitis or other episodes of illness. The hooves tell a story, like the rings in a tree trunk tell the age, thickness of growth in a year and climate changes.

When Happy first came to work with us at age 23 years, his hooves were in bad condition. A fungal infection, thrush had rotted his frog, which is a small area at the rear of a hoof that acts like a shock absorber. Happy's frog was so bad that the farrier almost put his hoof pick through. I soaked and sprayed his hooves in antibacterial and antiseptic wash, every day for a week and then every few days for month or so to kill the thrush. His frogs and hooves recovered and are as good as they can be for his age. Bob has little undulations on his hooves where he has

had bouts of laminitis. Bob is on the track system, so he has access to hay and not rich pasture. But sometimes Bob magically appears in the pasture as he sneaks through the hot tape.

To shoe or not to shoe? The therapy horses we work with are all bare hooved. Horses without shoes have increased proprioception, feeling of the ground where they step. We have been using a barefoot farrier who is a teacher of Equine Podiotherapy. This area of study applies knowledge of hoof anatomy and science for specialist hoof trimming.

Horseshoes were originally designed to stop the hooves of horses wearing away while horses were working on the roads delivering milk and ice. If you are interested, you can read about the benefits of bare hooves for horses at the Barefoot Blacksmith's website (barehoofcare.com).

Hooves and a track system

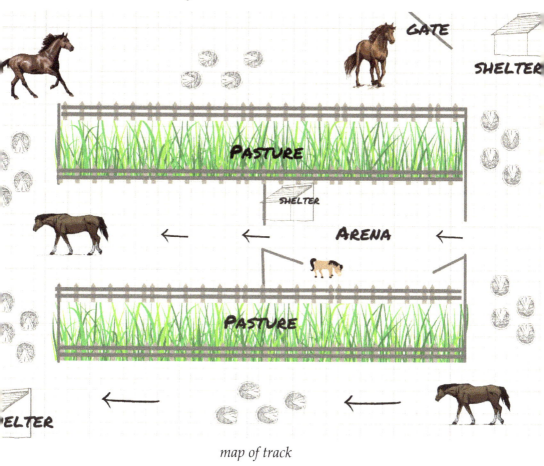

map of track

As horses are designed to move, the equine-assisted therapy centre is designed to use a track system for the horses. So, when they are not working, they are grazing and moving. There are areas under trees for scratching and shelters for protection from the sun and weather.

The arena is a walkthrough and part of the eight shaped system. There are different surfaces, such as rocks and logs around the system to keep the horses astute and sure-footed, especially around gates and areas that get muddy. There are many ideas for track systems and the book *Paradise Paddock: A guide to natural horse boarding* by Jaime Jackson is well worth a read.

Horses and grazing

Horses hooves and general health is impacted by what they graze on. In the area I work, farming and pastures were sown for cattle to graze. The pasture sown for cattle to graze generally has a higher sugar content. There are many varieties of grass with lower sugar content that are appropriate for horses to eat. Low sugar grasses help keep the weight of the horse down and serve well to reduce laminitis among other diet-related issues. We have used equine pasture mixes without rye grass and a variety of bent grass suitable for the area we work in. The type of grass that is suitable for your horses will depend on the area, temperature, climate and the soil PH.

Hay purchased and brought onto properties can have weeds that are not suited for horses. Pastures that have been grazed for a while may become mineral deficient. Introducing mineral blocks for your horses to access can support horse nutrient intake. If you do use mineral lick blocks, they can increase thirst. Horses should always have access to water. This is important as they can drink between 15–25 litres during the day. For example, there was a lack of magnesium in the soil where we work so we made sure there was access to mineral lick blocks and salt lick blocks for the horses to get more nutrients. Soil testing can help work out what condition the soil is in. This is an area where further research and learning is important for your therapy equine's health.

In addition to pasture grass and weeds, horses graze trees and bushes. They can eat a variety of plants, so be sure to check out what they can eat and what is poisonous to horses. Some people choose not to have trees in the paddocks where horses are. There is more information being published in this area and it is well worth familiarising yourself with it. Above is a photo of Trigger eating blackberries, he loves them. He also loves watermelon and bananas but we do not have these in the paddock. There is something naturally grounding about being outdoors in a paddock and listening to the herd rhythmically eat hay and watching them graze.

Horses and their teeth

A horse has between 36 and 42 teeth depending on gender. Equines are heterodontous, therefore they have different shaped teeth for different purposes. Horse teeth often wear in patterns, due to the way they eat their food, and these patterns are often used to estimate the age of the horse after it has developed a full mouth. Like humans, horses can develop a variety of dental issues.

When Bob first arrived at Harnessing Wellness, he still had his baby teeth. There was a day when I looked at him thinking something was strange, and I realised he had lost one of his front teeth. I thought he must have knocked it out but then he grew his adult teeth.

Trigger has two wolf teeth at the back of his mouth that can be removed if they cause him issues, and I was told if he was to be ridden with a bit, then it would cause pain and the teeth would have to be removed. So we learnt bitless riding.

Happy, being in his senior years, has regular check-ups by a horse vet dentist. This is a qualified vet who specialises in equine dentistry. The horses get a full health and dental check. Part of the full health check includes, for male horses, a sheath clean. The horse vet dentist cleans their sheath to reduce smegma and keep that part of the horse healthy. He told me once that in summer, that area of the horse can get infested by fly maggots, as it is warm. You should speak to your vet about this if you want to know more information. My horse trainer was particular about teaching us how to check and clean the horse's penis to reduce any health issues arising.

Horses have the largest eyes of all land mammals

Horses eyes are on the side of their heads. They have large eyes, the biggest of all land mammals in terms of its ratio to the size of their bodies. Humans are instinctively drawn to social connectedness and connection. Eye contact is a way humans communicate, as both inclusion and exclusion of another by gazing toward or looking away from another.[4]

Horses being stared at can interpret eye contact from the point of view of a prey animal – as being sized up for dinner. Although, looking into a horse's eyes is one way in which people may learn safe eye contact or 'being seen' by another, which can be important in building inclusiveness, a sense of self, and social connectedness. People can be drawn to horse's eyes and many will stare into them. I have seen horses turn their head away to reduce the intensity of eye contact and this observation is important. Remember, horses need to feel safe – if a human predator is looking directly at them, then it can make them uneasy. If a horse is untethered in a therapy session, they can walk away and enact what keeps them feeling safe.

Eye contact is one way horses make contact with others. It is also the process of getting permission to approach a horse. Exploring eye contact with horses, with their large, beautiful eyes and learning gentle eye contact in sessions, increases awareness of body language and social engagement cues. Asking, 'Let me know when you think they see you', 'When do they notice you?', or observing eye contact, can open up some interesting conversations about non-verbal communication, social dynamics and social boundary setting. Working with the horses is a way of engaging various conversations.

Following eye contact, the human brain's mirror neurons can search for social connection with the equine and unconditional positive regard is what a horse can offer in a therapy session. The

4. Koike T, Sumiya M, Nakagawa E, Okazaki S, Sadato N. 'What Makes Eye Contact Special? Neural Substrates of On-Line Mutual Eye-Gaze: A Hyperscanning fMRI Study.' *eNeuro.* 2019; 6(1). https://www.eneuro.org/content/6/1/ ENEURO.0284-18.2019 DOI: 10.1523/ENEURO.0284-18.2019

horse's nervous system attunes to a human and vice versa, as we both have mammalian brain structures and functions. This is part of why humans can feel calm following an interaction with horses and other mammals/animals who are settled and emotionally regulated.

I have been with nervous clients as they come into the paddock and when the horse notices them, the client observes. When both begin to relax, the person may breathe out and the horse may also breath out without conscious awareness that there is a shift toward relaxation and calm. This may be likened to attunement, where the nervous system and the somatic sense of safety and physiological restoration can begin to develop for people and horse alike in the moment. Breathing is a key element in the sessions and I teach clients how to breathe, to notice their breathing and work on self-soothing strategies to help settle their sympathetic nervous system.

Horses' ears and their story of attention

The ears of the horse have a lot to say. They are a focus for non-verbal communication. They flatten as a warning when the horse wants another horse or person to move away and space is needed. They stand to attention when focused. The ears of a horse give information as to the rest, relaxation, aggression, and the focus of the horse. They also increase the ability to attend to noise in the environment, and can move to attend to a noise without the head or eyes moving.

Horses' tails and manes

A horse's mane serves a couple of purposes. It acts as protection from insects and flies. It is also a source of warmth and protection and helps aid water run-off from the horse as well. Similarly, the horse's tail serves to protect the horse from losing heat around the underneath and back end. Like the mane, the tail is used to swish flies away from themselves.

Some horses stand head to tail with another in an act of mutuality, and to groom one another. The tail can be used to express non-verbal communication. It can flatten inward against the rump expressing fear or not wanting their tail to be picked up. It can be used to show irritation by swishing hard and fast. Furthermore, the tail can be raised to show excitement and energy.

Spending time around a horse's back end, scratching and touching their legs and brushing their tail increases their familiarity for people walking past. Bob used to turn and kick first when he got a fright, but I have spent a lot of time brushing and scratching and touching his hind legs for him to be more comfortable with people walking past and behind him. I now touch his back in sessions as I walk past and he appears more relaxed as people move around him.

Horses and touch

A horse can sense when a fly lands on their coat as it is highly sensitive. When socialising, horses touch to show their affection, such as using their nose, resting their head on the back of another horse, nudging each other and mutual grooming on each other's wither and other areas. A horse can be willing to be touched and also do the touching. They can lean into someone touching them and move away from touch in equine therapy sessions.

Observations of what horses like and where they like to be touched serves well. To ask permission to touch a horse is a polite gesture. Permission can be waiting for the horse to look at you, notice you and then be able to touch them. People can just touch horses without asking, and the response can be the horse walks away or flinches. Teaching respect with touch on horses does a number of things. It gives people the idea that they have to think before touching (increases awareness of impulses), it gives the horse a chance to orientate to the human, and it then gives both permission to be in the moment together.

As mentioned before, most horses enjoy connecting through touch, seeking contact and closeness. In building awareness and emotional regulation, we incorporate touch work to help ground and with the aim of becoming more present in the moment. Touching a horse in therapy can offer sensory experiences with different textures such as a muddy coat, clean tail, muscles, hooves, ears, muzzle and legs. It can be a way to learn about the horse and what they enjoy, the human can notice how the horse feels and how respectful touch can offer a mutual trust experience. Touching of hooves and legs can bring up fear for both the horse and human. When horses lift their hooves, they are giving you their life as it is more difficult to run away, so trust is imperative.

Horses and their body

The horse's body, even as a therapy horse, needs opportunity for exercise and fitness. Due to Trigger's curved spine, he had equine acupuncture. He was treated every few months by a vet who had further studied in spinal chiropractic and acupuncture. Acupuncture can help many conditions in the horse especially for the treatment of musculoskeletal pain. If Trigger is in pain, he will disengage. Because of the scoliosis in his back, this form of therapy has demonstrated to be of great benefit for him. This is where knowing your horse and their pain points can support their wellbeing in life and during their work in therapy sessions.

Horses and size

The size of a horse varies. The herd that I work with vary from 10 hands to 16.6 hands in size. Bob is the

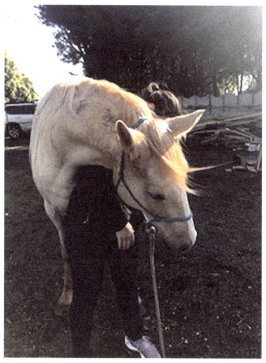

This is Trigger hugging his spinal vet.

smallest, being a Shetland cross miniature horse, standing at approximately 10 hands. Happy is an Australia Riding Pony standing at approximately 14.4 hands. Trigger is a warmblood Holsteiner x Sporthorse standing at 16.6 hands. Horses are measured in hands. One hand is 4 inches (101.16 mm) which is measured from the side of the hand, to the other side of the hand. Not from the palm to tips of fingers. Apart from Trigger coming into my world, I chose to work with horses

instead of other animals due to their size, their prey instinct, their huge heart space and their ability to attune to other mammals.

The size of a horse can be overpowering for some, but it is also something I believe draws people to them. They are visually appealing. The cuteness of Bob can be deceiving, as he is the cheekiest and the one I have to watch the most in equine-assisted therapy sessions. As he gets older, growing and developing his training needs are changing. Every interaction is a training opportunity. His inherent nature is gentle, he is curious and enjoys company. He needs more confidence in knowing what is expected of him and we are working on that. It is a good lesson for clients not to make assumptions about people and animals on face value.

Between the ears: the equine and human brain in summary

There are similarities and differences between human and equine brains. The human brain is able to reason, problem solve, plan and think in timelines past and present. The frontal cortex is an area for language, thought, problem solving, expression and self-awareness. It is also the area of the brain that has been shown to reduce activity and shut down when traumatic thoughts or memories are triggered.

The middle part of the brain, the limbic system (the mammalian brain) is where the emotional, traumatic memory, sensory memory and the amygdala reside. The amygdala sounds an 'alarm' if we are in danger. The amygdala and limbic system talk to the brain stem (reptilian brain), which is responsible for heart rate, temperature, and instinctive responses. The brain stem is where our survival responses for flight, fight and freeze are activated through adrenaline flooding the sympathetic nervous system.

The **horse's brain** is designed to manage balance and body functions focusing on large muscle coordination. The equine brain has key connections from their perception directly to movement (flight). They have keen senses. Their sight and hearing are attuned to danger cues in the environment. Their vigilance serves them well if danger is in close proximity as it attunes them to the environment.

In both horses and humans, the limbic system is the area in the brain that holds the emotional, relational and traumatic memory. The brain's limbic system works to keep us safe and orientated to danger. The limbic resonance system enables horses to attune to herd members: if one horse runs, the other feels the energetic vibration of fear and runs too. The horse's brain is not designed to reason through learning new skills. However, they learn through both positive and negative reward and association. Their brain is designed to be hypervigilant, hence the saying, 'Horses are anxiety on four legs.'

All mammals have a limbic system, their instincts, and the capacity for sharing emotional states arise from this part of the brain. Research has shown that horses are able to read facial expressions and are able to distinguish between angry and happy faces. It is postulated that, as a prey mammal, recognising threat is important for survival. Therefore, reading human expressions and sensing emotions such as anger evokes a stress response, part of a warning system that facilitates horses to anticipate negative human behaviour like rough handling.[5] Perhaps that is why Happy walks away when he can't understand the emotion and Trigger reared when the farrier was so rough with him.

In addition, studies have shown that horses do actually have their own facial features and 'smile'. A group of horses were groomed gently on the part of their body that they appreciated the most (called by some a 'bliss spot') with the groomer's hands only, while another group of horses were groomed in a standard way. They found that the horses who were individually groomed in their bliss spots with hands were more contact-seeking. It was reported that those who were groomed in this way also displayed facial features akin to 'a smile', suggesting wellbeing. Being able to recognise a horse's smile could lead to better welfare and horse-human relationships. I loved reading this research and this is why I have adopted a relaxation-first approach to training therapy horses. To build a connection, you need to engage them at the spot that they enjoy a scratch – and now there is research to support it.[6]

Working with horses in therapy for human wellness adds social, emotional, psychological and physical engagement

5. Smith AV, Proops L, Grounds K, Wathan J, McComb K. 'Functionally relevant responses to human facial expressions of emotion in the domestic horse (*Equus caballus*).' *Biol. Lett.* 2016; 12(2). https://royalsocietypublishing.org/doi/full/10.1098/rsbl.2015.0907
6. Lansade L, Nowak R, Lainé AL, Leterrier C, Bonneau C, Parias C, Bertin A. 'Facial expression and oxytocin as possible markers of positive emotions in horses.' *Sci Rep.* 2018 Oct 2;8(1):14680. DOI: 10.1038/s41598-018-32993-z. PMID: 30279565; PMCID: PMC6168541.

opportunities for clients. Horse and human brains (mammals in general) are wired for connection and relationship. Healthy relationships serve to buffer both humans and horses from loneliness and depression, as recent research has found. Evolution has meant horses and humans both have a keen ability to attune to

Horses can smile …

other members in their groups, herds and tribes for safety and comfort.

The benefit of engaging the limbic system with humans, in therapy outdoors with horses, is that it activates the brain chemistry and nervous systems, which can be affected by those closest to us. This is called **limbic resonance**.

In some cases, therapeutic contact (horse nose on the human cheek) can offer a safe sense of touch, a new experience to those who may have experienced domestic violence or little or no affection growing up. Through having new positive experiences with horses, people can develop a new understanding of a relational experience (limbic revision). Clients may be able to relax, for example, as they watch a horse quietly eat. Developmental psychology highlights the importance of healthy childhood relationships, that attachment with caregivers is fundamental for an individual to thrive. This attachment process and attunement to our needs has profound implications for the development of personality and lifelong emotional health (limbic regulation).[7]

Humans have both predator and prey instincts

Humans have both predator (fight) and prey (flight/flee/freeze) instincts, which can add a level of complexity to our lives and how we choose to behave in different scenarios – bullying in the workplace comes to mind. Horses do not connect with emotions of anger and frustration as they are not able to interpret or reason through predator instincts or those human emotions as mentioned above. Horses are honest in their behaviour – not unkind – and do what makes sense to them. As such, they can offer people a safe and healthy corrective emotional experience to discuss within and after therapy sessions.

I urge you to learn more about the brain, particularly the limbic system, or refresh your knowledge in this area to bring awareness to the horse and human brains and to further learn how you can integrate this knowledge into understanding how horses and humans process the world differently.

Regulating energy and the nervous system

Horses have a number of energy levels they cycle through, low energy (i.e. grazing), medium energy (i.e. from walking to trotting) and high energy (i.e. gallop). Horses are able to regulate themselves using movement. An example of the cycle of regulation is grazing, to being startled, to running away, to turning back and facing the fear, and then back to grazing.

---

7. Shah NS. 'Effects of Attachment Disorder on Psychosocial Development.' *Inquiries Journal*. 2015; 7(2). http://www.inquiriesjournal.com/articles/1667/effects-of-attachment-disorder-on-psychosocial-development

It has been postulated by Dr Peter Levine – the originator of Somatic Experiencing® with doctorate degrees in Medical Biophysics and Psychology, and the author of *Waking the Tiger* – that wild animals do not get post-traumatic stress. He researched how animals discharged their shock energy response since animals in the wild are constantly under threat and show no outward signs of trauma. He found that mammals have key survival instincts that keep them safe, and through regulating their nervous system, they are able to move through the incident without getting traumatic memory or energy 'stuck' in their nervous system and relive it again. This theory is of great support to the work with humans and horses for many reasons. One of which enables the person who has experienced something traumatic to understand the nervous system and why it holds traumatic energy in which we may develop behaviours to assist regulation like avoidance, anger, substance misuse, eating disorders and dissociation.[8]

Horses are sentient beings

Horses have been recognised as 'sentient' beings and the new ground-breaking legislations that recognise an animal's sentience is based on science and evidence in some parts of Australia.[9]

Animal sentience is the capacity for an animal to experience different feelings such as pain and pleasure. Horses can learn from experience and association. They live in awareness and

---

8. Levine P, Frederick A. *Waking the Tiger: Healing Trauma.* USA: North Atlantic Books; 1997.
9. RSPCA. 'RSPCA Australia welcomes new world-leading animal welfare legislation in the ACT.' RSPCA 2019. https://www.rspca.org.au/media-centre/news/2019/rspca-australia-welcomes-new-world-leading-animal-welfare-legislation-act

assess changes in the environment and can remember, process risks and benefits and then make a choice to meet their needs in the moment. In equine-assisted therapy sessions, having horses and ponies generally untethered, to freely walk around, enables them to choose to engage with the client or manage their interactions with clients. Therefore, in the therapy horse and pony training sessions, I generally talk with clients about how the therapy horses are trained. I believe this supports risk and safety management. I believe it also contributes to equine welfare and the cognitive concept and the development of the horse as a sentient being and not an object. It is a three-way approach: to support client, psychologist and horse safely.

This poem puts into perspective what being with and understanding horses is like.

The 10 Commandments for Horses

Anon

1. My life is likely to last 20 or more years. Any separation from you will be painful for me. Remember that before you take me home.

2. Give me time to understand what you want from me.

3. Place your trust in me. It is crucial to my wellbeing.

4. Don't be angry with me for long. Don't lock me up as punishment. You have your work, your entertainment and your friends. I … have only you …

5. Talk to me sometimes. Even if I don't understand your words, I do understand your voice when it is speaking to me.

6. Be aware that however you treat me, I'll never forget it.

7. Remember before you hit me that I am powerful enough to hurt you but choose not to.

8. Before you scold me for being uncooperative, obstinate or lazy, ask yourself if something might be bothering me. Perhaps I have a problem that you are not yet aware of.

9. Take care of me when I am old. You too will be old one day.

10. Go with me on the last journey. Never say, 'I can't bear to watch,' or, 'Let it happen in my absence.' Everything is easier for me if you are there …

Step Four

Herds for Health

Call it a clan, call it a network, call it a tribe, call it a family. Whatever you call it, whoever you are, you need one.

– Jane Howard

Herds and neuroception

Herds are social groups of prey mammals, generally of the same species that live together. As prey mammals, a herd offers resources for safety by having more eyes and ears to sense danger. Staying safe is neurobiologically wired into a mammal's brain, especially in a prey mammal, and neuroception is the process that describes how neural circuits in a mammal's brain assess whether something, someone or an environment is safe, dangerous or life threatening.[10] It is an instinctual process like a baby cooing when seeing a caregiver or crying when a stranger talks to them. Neuroception was a term coined by Dr Stephen Porges in his research of the nervous system and the development of the Polyvagal Theory.

---

10. Porges S. *The pocket guide to the polyvagal theory: The transformative power of feeling safe.* New York: W.W. Norton & Company, Inc; 2017.

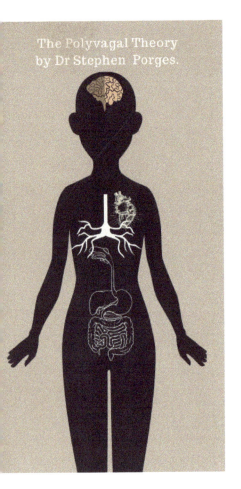

The Polyvagal Theory by Dr Stephen Porges.

VENTRAL VAGAL NERVE

- Social connection and engagement
- Nervous system location: Face, throat, chest area
- Ability to talk, engage, co-regulate, self-soothe and remain calm.

SYMPATHETIC NERVOUS SYSTEM

- Mobilisation for action- Fight & Flight
- Nervous system activity: Along the spinal cord to ready the body to fight or run away
- Physiological survival changes : Increased heart rate, tense muscles, fast shallow breathing.

DORSAL VAGAL NERVE

- Immobilisation/deactivate for survival, symptoms include freeze, collapse, dissociate.
- System activity is in the diaphragm, heart and gut
- Physiological survival changes to shut off from the threat when we can not fight or flight. Decreased heart rate, low energy, depressed, numb, shut down .

Horses in herds are happier

Horses in herds or with companion animals are generally happier and more engaged socially. Herds provide social interaction, reduce boredom and loneliness. Herd behavioural rules allow each horse to have some predictability which is supported by hierarchy. This offers safety, security, and comfort for a horse. Horses graze, groom, play and sleep better in the company of other horses.

When grazing, horses have their head down, their necks rotate and with their eyes located on the side of their head it increases their visual field. More horses mean more eyes and ears are paying attention to approaching danger. Survival behaviours, such as horses facing their paddock mates' hooves while grazing, enables them to stay alert while they eat and if they are under threat, it means they can run if their paddock mate runs. React first, think later.

Herd dynamics

In the wild, a herd environment would generally consist of a leader and followers. The follower horses are responsible to follow others as they are generally lower on the pecking order. The leader's responsibility is to guide the herd members to water, shelter and food. They also access those resources before the followers. As mentioned, horses are motivated by the safety in numbers of a herd, as it reduces their stress and increases their comfort from harm and predators. It also allows for better space and time to play and food as they graze for approximately 15 hours a day.

Both positive and negative reinforcement behaviours are used in a herd dynamic to establish hierarchy and govern consistent herd behaviour. Horses work out their hierarchy system by moving the other herd members' feet and walking into their physical space. They will share their shelter and food, for example, with horses lower on the pecking order and not in direct competition for their position in the hierarchy.

Trigger is a perfect example of this, he will not let Happy come into the shelter, but Bob can stand with him. We put up a shade sail for Happy to access relief from the sun when standing with the others. Trigger will also let Bob eat hard feed and hay with him, but Happy is not to go near him when he is eating. Additionally, Happy will not let Bob eat with him. Knowing these types of dynamics helps with planning therapy sessions. I rarely use food in sessions as I do not want to encourage the horses to make that association and nose around looking for food when clients arrive, especially with children; however, I have for the purpose of clinical intervention used food/hay in an activity around self-care and eating issues. Generally, I only have Trigger and Bob or Happy separately in a session when there is food.

In therapy sessions, another thing to observe is when horses move the client's feet, without the client knowing because the horse has determined that the client may be treated as lower in the hierarchy. I have worked with horses who are lower in their herd hierarchy, and they can try to dominate an unsuspecting client who does not understand horse language well. The moving of feet can provide a lovely learning experience for the client around setting physical and emotional boundaries for self-care. This behaviour of a herd can offer information in equine therapy sessions.

Domestic horses may have compromised natural herd instincts as they may have to function and live in unnaturally forced herd dynamics with limitations to space, age, gender, food supplies or they live in isolation in a paddock next to another horse. In therapy sessions, I work with the same herd members to understand the herd and individual members of the herd. Within that herd, different horses or ponies will step forward into the session. Others will walk away and do their own thing, but that is their choice, and it is respected.

Generally, horses that live in herds show less stress-related behaviours such as cribbing and weaving. Safety, comfort, play and food are the most important factors for a horse. When there is an imbalance of one of the factors, they will act it out. They will seek to be with others before they will eat. I have seen this within the Trigger, Bob and Happy herd when I take one for a walk down the road. It looks like Trigger and Happy are not close in the paddock, but they are each other's herd and if I take Trigger for a walk, Happy will run and call after him. I was very mindful of this and made sure Bob would be with Happy, and that Trigger and I went out on walks in a graded fashion so Happy worked out that Trigger would return. Trigger would call for Bob when we went for walks too. They do not like to be separated. They are each other's herd and being together makes sense to them.

Trigger, Bob, Bailey and myself sitting down for a rest.

If a horse does not feel safe, they will not seek comfort or rest such as lying down to sleep, nor will a food be a motivator. An example of this is when I take Trigger for a walk, I try to feed Happy prior to doing this to distract him, but it does not work. Happy's focus is on Trigger and his safety of being in the herd. I have heard people call it separation anxiety, a herd (even if it is one other horse) is safety for a horse and without them they do not instinctually feel safe.

Building internal and external psychological resources to cope assists horses and humans alike to calm the nervous system and reduce stress and enable them to think through things. Internal resources are experiences that support the mind and thinking processes. For humans, it can be pleasant thoughts, memories or dreams. For horses, it can be routine, familiarity and positive training experiences. External resources for humans may be things like nature, activities and physical fitness. For horses, it's similar with exercise and being outside in nature.

In simple terms, both humans and horses can access logic in the left side of the brain. It is regarded as the thinking brain, whereby humans and horses are more calm and less reactive. Humans experience the world differently. The right side of the brain has been described as the "rioting brain", it holds our creative ideas, instinctive responses and emotional reactions. The left side of the brain has areas for logical thought, problem solving, ability to carry on "normal" life after trauma.

Dr Daniel Siegal and Tina Payne Bryson wrote a book called *The Whole Brain Child* and it outlines these parts of the brain, as well as the growth and development techniques for assisting children move between the right brain using connection, redirection, and empathy. It also discusses parenting and relationships from a connection-based approach.

Pat Parelli, a horse trainer, used a similar type of analogy to work with horses. He would encourage people to get their horses to use the left side of the brain to be able to think and not react. However, he also found that there were many types of personalities with horses. It is an interesting concept to think about when working with horses and also that each horse has its own personality and motivations.

According to the Parelli Training Method, particular types of training and experiences can assist horses become more willing, calm, motivated and trusting. It is worth exploring for more ideas and philosophies, among other natural horsemanship training, to understanding horses and build their internal and external resources.

For humans, resources that settle the nervous system can be a comforting memory or an image of a previous experience such as walking along the beach or hugging a close friend. Social engagement with people we care about can also be a resource like a herd for horses. Social isolation for humans is a major source of psychosocial stress and is associated with an increased  prevalence of vascular and neurological diseases.[11]

Clients may choose to engage in equine-assisted therapy to connect with horses and understand herds, as humans are not a first choice due to abuse or other reasons. Psycho-education on herd respect dynamics and healthy social systems can assist a client with the idea of social contact and learn about safety cues to later engage with safe people. For clients working with

11. Friedler B, Crapser J, McCullough L. 'One is the deadliest number: the detrimental effects of social isolation on cerebrovascular diseases and cognition.' *Acta Neuropathol.* 2015 Apr;129(4):493-509. DOI: 10.1007/s00401-014-1377-9. Epub 2014 Dec 24. PMID: 25537401; PMCID: PMC4369164.

Here I am walking Trigger in hand on a soft lead.
He is following the feel of the rope and my body language.

herds, grounding and self-soothing exercises can be resourceful for them, with discussions around pleasant sensations, safe and welcoming touch, and grooming.

Horses bond and calm their nervous system through grooming each other. As a remedy and resource for reducing stress, isolation, fear and insecurity, it appears living in a herd is important for their wellbeing and a resource by way of attachment and bonding. I spend time scratching the therapy herd often. It is a way to do something for them without asking anything from them. I am the one to walk away to leave them wanting a bit more and they do seek it.

Here is Trigger at the end of a training session, playing with the 'carrot stick' which acts as an extension of your arm, providing a longer reach for communication.

Trigger eating the summer hat I had on during a training session.

Horses are very playful. When they feel safe and comfortable, they will play. I often set up an equine-assisted therapy session with plastic chairs to sit on to do some observation work. When I leave and return with the client, often the chairs will be tipped over – generally by Bob.

Photo of Bob in a group session, he is wearing Happy's halter so it is too big, but he is involved by keeping a cheeky watchful eye.

Herds and attachment as a resource

In human families, attachment begins in utero, and is a natural process made up of emotional, social, cognitive and physical connections an infant and young child has towards their primary caregiver. It is the foundation of all relationships. Bonding is reflective of the parent's connection towards the infant or child. A child who attempts to attach and be close to their mother, father or caregiver will use non-verbal gestures and behaviours such as smiling, physically holding on to the person, following them (i.e. crawl after them), putting their arms up in the air to be picked up, and some will make a sound or call out to be picked up.

In addition to attachment, there are other factors that can compromise understanding healthy relationships and safe people, such as emotional neglect experienced by a child from mis-attuned caregiving, abuse and neglect. Without a blueprint and an embodied sense of healthy attachment, a child may be more afraid of exploring new environments and will not initially identify safe supportive relationships.

For horses, similarly to humans, attachment and early socialising is the basis and blueprint of their interpersonal and relational development with other horses and humans. The main purpose for a horse is to attach and survive. Horses can be forgiving. Horses, when healthy, are excellent examples of self-care and have a natural sense of self-preservation. For horses, herd activities centre around establishing, building and nurturing relationships and there are important health benefits. Two horses biting at each other's withers, back, and rump areas to

Photo of Trigger and Bob eating.

Photo of Bob and Bailey playing.

groom serves as a social activity, reinforces social structure and builds companionships (you have to step into the space of the horse you're grooming). Horses also spend time together doing what looks like not much but it is their time together doing nothing and something that adds to their social bond.

Sometimes, horses will stand (top to toe) with their tail at the head of

Photo of Bob and Bailey standing with each other on a hot day.

the other horse and the other horse's tail will be at their head. This serves to swish flies off each other. It is another form of bonding and looking after herd companions.

Human-animal bond and interaction factors

The human-animal bond theory is based on a mutually beneficial and dynamic relationship between humans and animals. For the purposes of this book, I am referring to equines. The theory of the human-animal bond refers to modulated behaviours that are essential to the psychological, social, environmental and physical health and wellbeing of both the human and the equine.

Psychological attributes such as personality and empathy towards animals and people in equine therapy sessions is important in terms of the quality of interaction between the horse and the client.[12]

In therapy, the horse is a horse and acts as a relationship and social lubricant, it helps facilitate social interactions with the psychologist in a session. If the client is having difficulty with interpersonal skills, then the therapeutic intervention is the relationship between the horse and the client, and the discussions within the equine-assisted therapy session that offer a learning that can transfer skills into relationships in their daily life.[12]

Interesting research by Naber, Kreuzer, Zink, Millesi, Palme, Hediger, Glenk (2019), found that there were 'significant correlations between the therapist, client and horse were found with stronger interaction with familiar horse'. They also found

---

12. Scopa C, Contalbrigo L, Greco A, Lanatà A, Scilingo EP, Baragli P. 'Emotional Transfer in Human–Horse Interaction: New Perspectives on Equine-assisted Interventions.' *Animals* (Basel). (2019) Nov 26;9(12):1030. DOI: 10.3390/ani9121030. PMID: 31779120; PMCID: PMC6941042.

that the role of relationship quality within an equine assisted therapy session, showed synchronisation patterns with heart rate.[13]

Horses know their caregivers

Horses will attach to and know their people (caregivers). This is important to think about in terms of working with the same horses in therapy, training and caring for them too. Findings by Lampe and Andre (2012)[14] show that domestic horses were able to discriminate between familiar and unfamiliar human voices without using their sense of smelling or seeing. The way they set up their experiments led them to conclude that, 'the equine brain is able to integrate multisensory identity cues from a familiar human into a person representation that allows the brain, when deprived of one or two senses, to maintain recognition of this person.'

When you think of research like this, and apply it in terms of attachment, how many horses know their caregivers and then get moved on to someone else?

Safe physical contact between humans facilitates growth and attachment. Family therapist, Virginia Satir, quoted, 'We need four hugs a day for survival. We need eight hugs a day for maintenance. We need twelve hugs a day for growth.' Horses attach with paddock mates through grooming, grazing and shared activities of being together.

13. Naber A, Kreuzer L, Zink R, Millesi E, Palme R, Hediger K, Glenk L. 'Heart rate, heart rate variability and salivary cortisol as indicators of arousal and synchrony in clients with intellectual disability, horses and therapist during equine-assisted interventions.' *Pet Behaviour Science*. 2019, 17(23). DOI: 10.21071/pbs.v0i7.11801.
14. Lampe JF, Andre J. 'Cross-modal recognition of human individuals in domestic horses (*Equus caballus*).' *Anim Cogn*. 2012; 15: 623–630. https://doi.org/10.1007/s10071-012-0490-1

As mentioned before, horses in a herd are generally more settled. Grooming or brushing a horse before an equine-assisted therapy session can support relaxation and it gives both the horse and therapist time to connect before work begins, just as you would debrief with a colleague before running a therapy group. It is the physical touch and the body-to-body contact in some activities, such as hugging, brushing, leaning into the horse to emotional transfer between the human and the horse by way of experience that facilitates the bonding and in which the non-judgmental approach to their interaction can be felt.

Photo of scratching Happy and the enjoyment he gets from it.

How does touching or hugging horses compare to safe touch with humans? At this time, there is not much research to suggest that hugging a horse evokes oxytocin, but anecdotally some people do report they feel better. If a herd of horses have low energy and regulated nervous systems, people report that they feel more relaxed, and it can

Me scratching Trigger's ichy spot.

be postulated that it is through the process of attunement and neuroception. It may also be a combination of mindfulness of being with and observing a calm environment. Jon Kabat-Zinn, an expert in mindfulness-based stress reduction, defines mindfulness as 'awareness that arises through paying attention, on purpose, in the present moment, non-judgmentally.'

The herd interactions between humans and horses set the environment of a therapy session. There are a few things that horses in equine therapy sessions need to know through

Bob and Bailey spending time.

our actions and relationship. Those things include indications that humans are not going to hurt them, that they are not allowed to hurt us, that they can trust our decisions, and that they can be guided by us as the facilitator, especially when we are working at liberty in equine-assisted therapy.

These understandings are supported by the intention behind the actions. As horses watch body language to determine the intention of the human, they can be informed by their history of human interactions, handling, and adverse training methods. Harsh training methods for horses working as a therapy horse have no place in equine-assisted therapy. A horse trained by fear or fear-inducing methods on the behalf of the trainer or

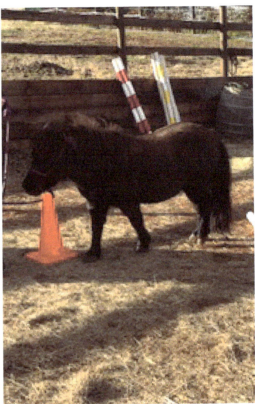

the facilitator, is likely to inform the horse what they can expect from human interactions perpetuating the prey and predator dynamic.

The horses who are fearful of humans will act in flight. If it is a fear-based experience, then the horse learns to 'do' an activity by fear. If it is a positive reward, then the horse learns the activity as a nice experience. So, it is about the handler, not the horse, and understanding horse psychology and behaviour in therapy sessions are invaluable learning, teaching safety and communication tools. The relationship between the therapist and the client includes role modelling and teaching respectful horsemanship skills.

I have realised over the years that it would be beneficial for the herd I work with to have similar re-training by the same horse trainer, using relaxation-first training methods, so all horses understand the same cues. In the herd I work with, there have been horses who have had careers as dressage and riding ponies, before their new career in therapy sessions. Having the same training on the ground enables them to understand the same requests from me and this allows me to guide inexperienced handlers. It reduces confusion for the herd members too when asked to do something.

Do not hit the horse, be observant

Abuse occurs in all facets of life unfortunately, and as previously mentioned, I have seen abusive behaviour and language used towards horses. I have been present when a person helping to facilitate an equine-assisted therapy session hit Bob, the little Shetland. He put his muzzle near her leg. Hitting a horse is about the person's lack of attention in the moment to the horse, a lack of skills, and not the horse. It may also be the person's lack of ability to communicate their intention with the horse or of being observant to the horse's behaviour. Hitting a horse in a therapy session is just a NO. There is no excuse, the person simply does not know how to speak or read the horse's body language.

Herd as an embodied sense of safety

- **Observation**

Observing and learning from a distance about healthy horses and herd dynamics can offer people an understanding of how healthy attachment may look in the horse world, as well as human. Healthy herds, herd hierarchy and bonding-grooming behaviours offer conversations for people who have not observed or experienced secure attachment and relationships with people. In equine-assisted therapy sessions, identifying with horses or ponies as 'non-judgemental' can offer the idea of an unconditional positive regard. Carl Rogers (1902–1987), a founder of humanist psychology, was known for developing the psychotherapy method called 'client-centred therapy'. Client-centred therapy was part of therapeutic rapport, without it you cannot do beneficial psychological counselling or equine-assisted therapy.

- **Safety with the herd**

We arrange for a safe place to be available for the client, whether it is the barrels to 'protect' the client or to climb through the safe fence and wait near a tree. In my experience, engaging people from complex backgrounds, especially those from complex living arrangements with abuse, in equine-assisted therapy can trigger their hypervigilance to danger. So, having a place to go to if they feel unsafe allows them to take control, to enact a process they might not have been able to during any previous abuse. I know clients watch my interaction with the horses first before they trust me. So, I talk about the horses and teach them about self-care, the brain, nervous system and the horse. They watch how the horses and ponies – the herd members – treat each other too.

If you work with young people, some may find it supportive in a session to create a "safe" place. This can aid in play and role modeling safety and open up discussions around safety plans.

- **Who moves whose feet and invades space determines the hierarchy**

Herd members move each other's feet, it allows them to invade space and determines who is higher in the hierarchy. This is important as horses in therapy sessions do it to clients and once the horse has established the hierarchy with an unsuspecting client, they may treat the client as lower in the herd. If we start thinking like a horse in an equine-assisted therapy session, the horse may be curious of the client and their place in the herd. There are no equal members in a herd – everyone has their place. Therefore, first, what the horse or pony wants to know is whether the client going to lead the horse and herd to survival resources such as water, shelter and safety, or will the horses themselves have to lead the person to those things to help them survive?

Do they move your feet or do you move theirs? A horse yielding to gentle pressure (ask them to move backwards) or setting boundaries (using the hand to stop the horse) with non-verbal cues are both helpful strategies. As the horse person in the equine-assisted therapy session, it is your role to watch the horses' behaviour and make sure the client is safe. Watching feet movement has been a helpful activity for people understanding boundary setting, especially those who have been bullied or in other areas in which they have been 'pushed around', and those impacted by early trauma, whereby their sympathetic nervous system – flight, fight, freeze responses – are activated. In sessions, observing and noticing herd and horse behaviour, practising awareness of safety, finding safe places, and working increased self-resilience helped develop anecdotal therapeutic

benefits. It can show how clever someone has been to minimise risk and give them some self-esteem and empowerment.

- **Horse senses within the herd**

In equine-assisted therapy sessions, the observation of horses can bring our focus on the horse's invitation into their space or understanding if the horse is uncomfortable. For example, their ears offer feedback. Attentive: both ears forward; listening: ears cocked; at rest: they are flopped; upset or angry: ears are pinned back. Horses can see and hear about a kilometre in front to the side and behind them. They are acutely aware of their environment. They use ten muscles to turn their ears. Watch the ears, they will tell you and your client a lot and which direction the horse is paying attention. Observation of herd members, for example, yawning is a form of stress reduction and a clenched jaw is a tense horse.

Horses can hear a human heartbeat from 1.2 metres away. When in a herd the horses synchronise their heartbeats and if one horse's heart beat goes up, they know there is danger. The findings of the research conducted by Keeling, Jonare and Lanneborn (2009) indicate that the heart rate of a rider and horse simultaneously increased under different experimental handling or riding conditions.[15] Furthermore, research by Linda Keeling suggested a horse can hear a heart beat from 4 feet away. They synchronise their heartbeats for safety. It could be assumed horses may also synchronise to our heartbeats to humans and our various emotional states, so if we are anxious around our horse they may become more nervous too.

Therefore, to support your therapy horses, keep things as familiar as possible unless they are well-adjusted to change, and teach them the same cues and body language to read to reduce stress for them. When a client who is inexperienced in horse handling and leading the therapy horse or pony, I always advise them to hold the rope loosely in their hands, like holding a pizza box or having a smile in the rope. And if they get worried or the horse or pony runs, then we drop the rope and say, 'See you later," and wave at them. Remember that your therapy horse looks to you, their person and facilitator for direction, and the most helpful thing you can do is to breathe and stay calm.

Subtle signs indicate how the herd member is coping or finding the interactions with a client. Knowing how to read a horse's body language in a herd is imperative, it can also help the client learn about horse behaviour and they can track it to see how the horse is doing to offer an altruistic activity to the therapy session. Generally, horses without their own traumas are naturally in a homeostatic state and return to it after going through their energy cycle.

---

15. Keeling LJ, Jonare L, Lanneborn L. 'Investigating horse-human interactions: the effect of a nervous human.' *Vet J*. 2009 Jul;181(1):70-1. DOI: 10.1016/j.tvjl.2009.03.013

They fluctuate through low energy, medium energy and high energy. Horses have a good shake and roll to reduce stress and will move toward their herd mates for comfort as a resource.

Finally, I have found integrating herds into a therapy session may not always go according to plan and change depending on the weather. Herd members may fare better on wet, windy days or sleep most of a hot day in summer. Individually, they may feel different due to the heat, rain and cold. The conditions of the area I work in can change from really muddy to dry. Sometimes, the horses do not feel like they want to participate and as much as I respect that the horses make those choices themselves, sometimes the client can take it personally. Everything that happens in the session is therapeutic information, if the client notices and begins talking about it.

I have let horses out of the arena mid-session, if they are standing by the gate or not settling. If a horse does not want to be led, we can change horses with a discussion that might explore what we think the horse might be feeling, or we check the wellbeing of the horse, i.e. touch their hooves, check their heartbeat, which can double as psycho-education into the importance of self-care and coping. Working with a consistent herd enables you to understand the dynamic of their hierarchy and help look after them, the clients and yourself in sessions. It also ensures safety in sessions, as you are aware of who may move whose hooves and enables planning sessions and activities.

Learning about horses is a life skill and journey, and just like people, everyone is different. Working as a practitioner in equine-assisted therapy is an ongoing learning process.

Step Five

Professional Responsibility

I often tell people in my clinics; the human possesses the one thing that means more to the horse than anything in the world, and that is peace and comfort.

– Buck Brannaman

As Buck Brannaman says, providing horses safety and comfort should be the aim for all practitioners who offer equine-assisted therapy services to both humans and horses. Codes of professional practice guide any registered mental health practitioner, including the services they offer the public. Thus, the integrity, ethical practices and professional responsibility is on the practitioner to make sure they do the right thing by the public, their clients, the profession and people referring clients to equine-assisted therapy services.

At the time of writing this book, there are no government regulations or standards for people offering equine-assisted therapy, and as such no consistent registered standards of practice in Australia. People who are not registered mental health professionals, with no mental health governing bodies, need to be clear about what they can offer their clients and determine their scope of professional practice and their legal obligations.

The danger of misrepresenting professional skills and practising outside of the scope of skills and training can be potentially damaging to the psychological and physical wellbeing of the clients, horses and the person offering their services. The following example is one of the prompts for this book to be written. This is something I heard through the grapevine and not the only case I have heard. A person offering equine-assisted work, not a registered mental health professional, was working with a 'traumatised' client. During a session with a client, the horse had done something the equine-assisted facilitator had not liked and in front of the client they backhanded their 'therapy' horse in the face. This is troublesome and disturbing on many levels. Needless to say, it reinforced to the client that violence was able to happen to both people and now animals. This is not trauma-sensitive, not animal-welfare friendly nor an example of good practice for equine-assisted therapy or therapy in general.

To offer best practice mental health interventions, research studies need to be conducted to identify that the intervention outcome can be replicated, that the intervention will do no harm to the client and it is the best chance of mental-health benefit to the client. To work outside of one's expertise and training increases risk to clients, the facilitator and the outcome of the therapy.

Building rapport with a client supports the therapeutic process and although someone might want to do equine-assisted therapy, it is still the therapeutic rapport between the therapist and the client that supports the change and therapeutic process. I aim to build a level of rapport that I would in a traditional therapy setting. The interventions I work with in equine-assisted therapy sessions with clients are determined by a treatment plan and the evidenced-based intervention informed by replicated research studies and thus recommended to psychologists. I do not make up my treatment plan based on merely what I think. It is informed through my training to understand and to choose the appropriate best-practice mental-health interventions.

In addition to belonging to professional associations and regulating bodies of professional codes of conduct, there are other guideline frameworks that support the professional responsibility in equine-assisted therapy. Equine-assisted therapy sessions need to be timed, managed and designed for the wellbeing of all those involved. Hausberfer, Roche, Henry and Visser found that there were three factors that impacted a horse's willingness to interact with a human. First, the nature, quality and frequency of contact with people. This is a good reminder for breaks between sessions, and being your horse's advocate and preparing the client to be appropriate with the horses. The second factor identified was the time period, and the third social environment.[16] Hence why I focus on having a herd to work with to support the horses in the session.

Furthermore, Work Safe Australia has guidelines for working with inexperienced people and horses and the Five Domains for animal welfare.[17] I go into these in more detail in later chapters. Be clear about your area(s) of expertise, and what you can offer for the safety of yourself, your clients, the horses and others.

---

16. Hausberfer M, Roche H, Henry S, Visser EK. 'A review of the human–horse relationship.' *Applied Animal Behaviour Science.* 2008; 109(1): 1-24. DOI:10.1016/j. applanim.2007.04.015
17. Mellor DJ. 'Operational Details of the Five Domains Model and Its Key Applications to the Assessment and Management of Animal Welfare.' *Animals* (Basel). 2017 Aug 9;7(8):60. DOI: 10.3390/ani7080060. PMID: 28792485; PMCID: PMC5575572.

The Five Domain Model Physical and Functional Domain Mellor (2017).
Survival – related factors (nutrition, environment and health)

Nutrition		Environment	
Restrictions:	Opportunities	Unavoidable/ imposed conditions	Available conditions:
Water intake	Drink enough water	Thermal extremes	Thermally tolerable
Food intake	Eat enough food	Unsuitable substrate	
Food quality	Eat a balanced diet	Close confinement	
Food variety	Eat a variety of food	Atmosphere pollutants: CO_2, dust and smoke	Suitable for freer movement
Voluntary overeating	Eating correct qualities		Fresh air
Force feeding		Unpleasant/ strong odours	Pleasant/ tolerable odours
		Light: inappropriate intensity	Light intensity tolerable
		Loud otherwise unpleasant noise	Noise exposure acceptable
		Environmental monotony, ambient, physical, lighting	Normal environmental variability
			Predictability
		Unpredictable events	

Health		Behaviour	
Presence of:	Little or no:	Exercise of 'agency' impeded by:	'Agency' exercised via:
Disease: acute, chronic, injury, chronic, husbandry mutilation	Disease or injury	Invariant, barren environment (ambient, physical biotic) Inescapable sensory Impositions Choices markedly restricted	Varied, novel engaging environmental challenges Congenital sensory inputs Available Engaging choices
Functional impairment: due to limb amputation, to lung, heart or vascular kidney, neural, or other problems.	Functional impairment Poising Body condition Appropriate	Constraints on environment Focused on activity Constraint on animal-to animal Interactive	Freedom for movement Exploration Foraging / Bonding reaffirming Rearing young
Obesity / leanness Poor physical fitness: muscle de-conditioning	Good fitness level.	Limits on threat avoidance, escape or defensive activity Limitations on sleep and rest	Playing Sexual activity Using refuges, retreat

Affect Experience Domain		Mental Wellbeing Domain	
Negative	Positive	Negative	Positive
Thirst Hunger (general) Hunger (salt) Malnutrition malaise Bloated over full Gastrointestinal pain	Wetting / quenching pleasure of drinking Pleasure of different taste / smells / textures Pleasure of salt tastes Masticatory pleasures Post prandial satiety Gastrointestinal comfort	Pain, forms of discomfort Thermal: chilling Overheating Physical: joint pain, skin irritation Physical; stiffness muscle tension Respiratory e.g. Breathlessness, Olfactory Auditory: impairment, pain, Visual: glare / darkness / eye strain Malaise from unnatural constancy	Forms of comfort Thermal Physical Respiratory Olfactory Auditory Visual

Negative	Positive	Negative	Positive
Breathlessness			Calmness
		Anger, frustration	Engaged in control
Pain: many type		Boredom, helplessness	
S			Affectionate sociability
		Loneliness, isolation	
Debility, weakness	Comfort of Good health and high functional capacity	Depression	Maternally rewarded
Sickness, malaise		Sexual frustration	Excited playfulness
Nausea			Sexual gratification
Dizziness		Anxiety	
	Vitality of fitness	Fearfulness,	Secure/protected /confident
		Panic,	
Physical exhaustion		Anger, Neophobia	Likes novelty
		Exhaustion	
			Energised / refreshed

Step Six

The Horse is Not the Therapist

If you cannot measure it, it does not exist.
– Brene Brown

My equine-assisted therapy practice adheres to the same professional psychology codes and protocols that I work within when I see someone in a traditional room-based psychology session. I discuss the client's consent, rights to privacy and confidentiality, discuss fees and talk through the paperwork for them to give informed consent and sign the documentation for us to enter into a therapeutic relationship. The parameters of the therapeutic relationship, circumstances in which breaching confidentiality is necessary, are also discussed and require consent. For children and adolescents who require a parent or guardian to consent on their behalf, I go through the same details with the young person and their parent/s or guardian/s.

Additional equine-assisted therapy paperwork is administered for people who wish to do equine-assisted therapy. I discuss this paperwork and talk about horses, their non-verbal behaviour and the risks involved, such as the horse is a flight animal that will revert to their natural instincts to protect themselves. Parents are also present when it is a child that they are consenting for therapy and all of the above information is explained and has to have informed consent by way of a signature from the parent or guardian and client. I too sign the consent form. A background history is taken before we meet the horses, and therapeutic goals discussed so I can begin formulating a psychological treatment plan.

Before the client touches a horse, we observe the horses so we can discuss them. It gives some insight into how the client sees and understands horses, their anxieties and impulsive behaviour. I start to teach the client about the horse's body language and how horses communicate. I may repeat this and I often refer to a slow 'moon walk' that younger people, especially those who have impulse-control issues, are invited to adopt to assist in reducing the likelihood of the horses getting startled. Working with inexperienced people around horses requires additional awareness from the psychologist-practitioner.

Professional regulation associations and governing bodies for psychologist and mental health practitioners should be adhered to. There are Acts and Legislations that guide working with inexperienced people new to handling horses. Specifically in Australia, they are called Australia Horse Safety. However, there are other guidance bodies too.

These regulations are essential to incorporate into your policies and standards of equine-assisted therapy practice with horses, as they are used by Worksafe to investigate incidents in the workplace and used as guides for legal proceedings. Being aware of these regulations, or those in your state or country, assists in being practical in working with horses in therapy.

The horse is not a therapist

A great therapist is: According to Dr Peter Levine, Ph.D., "Presence. The ability to remain centred and resonate in a primitive way with your clients. The ability to connect with their inner world, nervous system to nervous system. Let difficult feelings and sensations move through you, showing your client how to feel their feelings, and then let them go. Do your own work so you can resonate emotionally. The treatment modality is only 15% of therapy, and 85% is the relationship you develop together."

The horse is not the therapist, it does not facilitate therapy sessions, and the horse is not the co-therapist. The horse is a horse; the pony is a pony; and the donkey is a donkey. They are present in the process of therapy, they themselves are being an equine. What is lovely about having equines in therapy sessions can be many things depending on what is helpful and engaging to the client. Horses and ponies vary in size, colour, coat texture, heartbeat, eye colour, hooves, tails, manes, their curiosity and the affection, and their low, medium and high energy levels. Their survival responses and their behaviour are a wonderful way to understand self-care or how we see ourselves in our world. A horse walking away from a client, who really wants the horse to come to them, may offer a projection or learning about relationships, self-esteem or it may open up a difficult conversation such as, 'The horse doesn't like me like the kids at school, they walk away from me too.'

In the paddock with the horses, I continue to work as a psychologist using evidenced-based interventions, weaving the way of the horses into the conversation through metaphor, projection or psycho-education of symptoms and narrative.

Being outdoors gives the client freedom to move, which can help regulate their nervous system. They can run away or move toward the horse depending on their feelings – something they may not be able to do if they were assaulted or abused. Horses are straightforward in their relationships and building rapport. They do not judge, they do not blame and they will not tell the secrets told to them. Horses can offer a non-judgemental relationship where you can practise building trust. Over time, that experience may be applied to safe human relationships too.

Building rapport is the centre and the focus of interventions being effective. The horses bring the sessions back to basics: what joy and a smile a horse passing wind can bring to a session, especially for someone who cannot open up in a 'clinical' setting. Feedback has come back from parents or workers about the fact that the client has engaged, and they believe it is because of the space and the interactions with the horse that have been novel, less intimidating or confronting than in a clinical room. Walking and talking is something most people can do and this combination benefits people physically and psychologically.

The following are psychology interventions and therapies (not extensively) that have been highlighted as best-practice evidence-based psychological therapies at the time of writing this book. I have listed these therapies as I have trained in and applied these as therapeutic frameworks to underpin my treatment and interventions in equine-assisted psychology sessions.

Psycho-education

Giving psycho-education about mental health symptoms begins with a client after the intake assessment. Like room-based psychological sessions, psycho-education is an intervention and discussion about mental health symptoms. Psycho-education of the mental health diagnosis are intertwined into the experience of being with the horses, and sometimes projected onto the horse to explore how the horse may experience the symptoms and how the client may experience their symptoms. Happy the pony, experienced grief, pain and depression. When he first arrived to work with us, he had left his paddock mate of ten years and had bad thrush in his hooves. He would stand by the tree and not eat much. Trigger is a prime example of an anxious horse, who can react to something before thinking; for example, Trigger does not understand what wheelbarrows or prams are and they scare him. We discuss the horses and their personalities and predispositions.

Formulating treatment plans around predisposition, precipitating and perpetuating factors are discussed in client appropriate language. Individuals are helped to understand their symptoms to explore coping strategies. The horses are a social lubricant, they may break up the formality of the information delivery and can add comfort by way of touch or being there holding space. Part of the

session includes how clients can learn to separate themselves from the symptoms to increase their wellbeing and assist them harnessing their psychological wellness.

Utilising Interpersonal Therapy (ITP) as an intervention for people with depression works well with the horses. Given the spectrum and various levels of acquaintances, friends and family relationships, working with a horse herd opens up avenues to overt discussions and observations of relationship dynamics and how challenging relationships may cause distress for the client. Focusing on interpersonal relationships and improving interpersonal functioning and social supports can be highlighted through the work with the horses and the herd. Working with the horses and the activities encourages movement, and also learning herd dynamics can increase understanding and projection of one's own interpersonal interactions. Herd dynamics can offer a way to explore interpersonal issues, expectations of relationships, social support and communication skills. Being with the horses can offer an opportunity for interspecies connection too.

Solution-Focused Brief Therapy (SFBT) places importance on discussing solutions to the client's problems in the present, rather than the way the client's past has influenced them at the time. Clients attend with a problem, and the problems can be worked through with the horses. In sessions, the client is welcome to build obstacle courses that may represent a problem, explore what it looks like in 3D, choose a horse to walk through or around the obstacle and  discuss the process as they go. The horses sometimes become part of the problem and working out how to manoeuvre them or coax the horses or ponies through the obstacle can be part of the problem-solving.

Schema-Focused Therapy (SFT) employs basic cognitive behavioural techniques to identify and change belief systems, automatic thoughts, identify cognitive distortions, and explore an individual's maladaptive rules about how to survive in an environment created from their belief systems.

Activities with the horses, such as the development of a moral compass can occur as the client may be invited to do an activity to show care to the horse; for example, help pick hooves, or feed and water the horses. The client may perceive himself as having a purpose and derive fulfilment from this activity. EAP activities such as 'Halter and Lead' or 'Grooming' the horse can also support a client in finding a purpose to participate in a task-focused activity and be part of the outcome, i.e. a clean pony or relaxed horse. Experiential equine-assisted therapy work includes creative experimental activities, to walk and talk through various belief systems, to challenge the beliefs with positive experiences and the validation from the clinician and the horse.

Emotion-focused activities deal with emotions caused by a stressor. During activities in equine-assisted therapy the client may find they are confronted by their emotions present during the activity, i.e. feeling overwhelmed or scared. This raises awareness and a platform to explore the development of the client's current symptoms, exploring and processing memories of any aversive childhood experiences.

The relationship between the psychologist and the client has the potential to be a corrective emotional experience and the horses may assist in this process by being present and offering a horse-human connection. Exploring techniques can be employed to challenge difficult emotions, negative self-talk and other maladaptive schemas using experiential interventions with horses such as walking over poles or building obstacle courses. Challenging belief systems may become apparent by someone thinking they could not lead such a big horse or feel safe, or having a choice in the interaction. Self-belief of being able to have influence in life is challenged by activities with the horses that involve problem-solving to achieve an outcome. We can work on challenging belief systems by doing activities to explore the reasoning behind the schema and then work on new ways to meet core emotional needs.

Cognitive restructuring: The treatment activity goal is to identify and modify thought and belief patterns that contribute to a client's emotional and behavioural dysfunction. Search for evidence for and against a particular thought pattern, like 'I am not good at anything.' Equine-assisted therapy activities create an opportunity for the client to bring their thinking and meaning related to their current or previous life challenges to observations with the horses and horse-related activities, and search for the evidence that supports and/or does not support the thinking. You are not able to trick a horse or a pony, they can sense the level of activation in someone's nervous system. As mentioned, horses are able to read human facial expressions, although they do not understand anger or disgust. If you are skilled in reading horse's body language, chances are you are given a hint about how the client is going. For example, if the horse is agitated, then there is a likelihood the client is high energy too. Always be curious.

Behavioural practice: The equine-assisted therapy treatment goals focus on behaviour and exposure to situations designed to promote mastery and increase self-esteem. Horses add warmth to the sessions with their unconditional positive regard. Being overly warm and familiar also has its issues so learning to balance somewhere in-between and setting boundaries is also important when being with the horses. Working with horses with or without words, horses will make it clear when someone is crossing their comfort space bubble and identifying boundaries will become obvious. Through different equine-assisted therapy activities, the clients practise small changes in behaviour to achieve the desired goal; for example, leading the horse and setting physical boundaries. Emotional regulation tends to be part of the treatment plan. Trigger is a big horse and some people find him intimidating and can be scared by his size. Trigger used to be scared of plastic bags and this story can be quite funny for people who are scared by him. Overcoming that initial fear and learning to work alongside Trigger or Happy and even Bob builds confidence.

As mentioned, these are a few evidence-based practice theories but others can be applied as a theoretical underpinning to explain your treatment focus and plan and how you incorporate the horses in various interventions. In order to write up the client case notes and client formulations, you need to understand your evidenced-based intervention

and theory that supports your interventions with that client.

Additional mental health outcomes include self-care such as exercise for mental wellbeing. Exercise appears to increase brain plasticity and enhance ability to learn from and adapt to stressful situations. Equine-assisted therapy activities are generally outside and require physical movement and exercise. Most sessions start with observation of the horse and a discussion around their behaviour and how they might feel. This is to increase the client's awareness of non-verbal body language of the horse, to allow the horses to become aware of us in their space and look for permission to engage.

Horses have a lot to teach us about the value of physical and mental effort, and useful lessons in all aspects of life. Furthermore, the benefits of appropriate social support can be found in groups. Connecting with the horses in a peer group can decrease loneliness, reduce risk-taking behaviour, increase feelings of self-worth, and help a person put problems into perspective. The group setting enables clients to reflect that others have similar issues, and this also can reduce feelings of isolation, normalise symptoms and see horses as sentient beings (extends the notion of animal welfare).

Step Seven

Setting Safety Guidelines

If you want to improve the world,
start by making people feel safer.

– Dr Stephen Porges

The statistics from Safe Work Australia at the time of writing are that one person a day in Australia is hospitalised due to a horse-related injury. Safety is not only physical, but also emotional, intellectual, and spiritual.

Dr Stephen Porges, author of *The Polyvagal Theory*, emphasises a link between psychological experiences and physical manifestations in the body. The Polyvagal Theory postulates that through evolution, the human-mammals neural circulates, the autonomic nervous system expresses different adaptive behaviour in terms of defensive strategies.[10] First, we can mobilise our bodies to either fight or flight/flee, or hide or freeze (feign death). In the brain at the same time, the frontal lobe responsible for problem-solving has decreased activity and the limbic system has increased activity, whereby the amygdala sends an alarm (adrenaline) down the brain stem and into the nervous system to activate to flight, fight, submit or freeze. There is another survival instinct, a defence mechanism, that I thought worth mentioning here, called fawning. Fawning is an instinctual behaviour of 'people-pleasing' that is used to diffuse conflict and reduce harm from a perpetrator or perceived threats. It is a clever way to survive when the others are not an option. Being aware of survival defence mechanisms is a foundation to supporting clients to feel safe in equine-assisted psychology sessions.

One way to establish emotional safety in an equine-assisted psychology session is to observe the herd. The skill of observation is important to notice our surroundings, people and animals within our environment. It is a skill that can inform us if someone or something is not safe. All prey-mammals observe, they stop and attend to their environment to get more information if there is a predator in the environment. Humans have both prey and predator instincts, which makes humans quite complex. To bring awareness of observation into the session begins to tap into that survival instinct. While observing the horses we can explore the non-verbal behaviour of the horse and the ways in which the horse communicates.

Something I find most interesting is that social behaviour is defined by the face and the heart connection, in which the neural regulation of the facial muscles and head are neuro-physically linked to the regulation of our heart.[10] Horses have a large heart space and limbic system. Therefore, part of the safety in setting up equine-assisted therapy sessions is to be conscious about social interaction and self-regulation. This aims to support a neurologically safe environment. Another way to work towards a regulated herd is familiarity with each other and the therapist – they know each other, they know the venue, and they do not introduce anything new in sessions. In this way, the horses can regulate and assist the client to regulate by not reacting in flight mode.

Do no harm. Therapeutically, the clients, psychologists, therapists and the horses require safety to be able to work, change and grow though this mode of therapy. The horses are working at the time they enter the arena, they are doing a job, not just hanging out. The horses should be aware of the change and be able to do their job, by keeping themselves safe and knowing they are not to harm others. Equine-assisted therapy sessions need to be safe for everyone involved. Bob is 140 kilograms, so his kick does hurt. Trigger is 650 kilograms, and if he stood on your foot or tried to kick, there would be harm done.

Here are further guidelines that I use for managing and implementing equine-assisted psychology sessions at Harnessing Wellness. There are a number of factors that over the years I have found very important in setting up the Equine-assisted Therapy Clinic. Topics here include: horses, their training, venue, legislations, weather, natural disasters and the client.

Guideline 1: Horse and pony training

After working with horses in therapy for a few years, I decided reading non-verbal behaviour was not enough, I wanted to learn about equine psychology. I found an equine psychology and behaviour course that went for a year and a half. I found it to be insightful and helpful and it changed the way I understood and worked with horses. It improved my holistic approach to horse husbandry, training and integrating them into therapy. I employed two horse trainers, both gentle, with relaxed methods of training and who focused on the horse's wellbeing.

I felt it was important for the horses I worked with to understand similar cues. They all had different owners, different experiences, and training prior to working with me, and due to their temperament and history of learning, I needed a common method to communicate with them. The horse trainer helped me train the horses the same way at liberty and to respond to visual cues to stop, come and walk around, using my body and hands as visual cues.

I have expectations of what my horses and ponies do in their role in equine-assisted therapy, just like expectations for a horse or pony in the dressage arena or horses involved in eventing. I have them trained so that they are familiar with their therapy-horse role on the ground with people, and I know mine and we can communicate and work together. It also helps me teach clients, who are generally inexperienced, in equine-assisted therapy sessions to handle the horses in a way the horses understand. I do not expect that a client would know how to put a halter on the horse, for example, so my therapy horses and ponies are able to cope with those types of situations.

My aim for the pony or horse would be that they can stand still while the client works through the process of trying to put the halter on. This comes down to playing with the horses and ponies, and putting ropes and things all over their bodies, and them learning they are okay while this happens. For example, I have had a client who was problem-solving and turned the halter upside down to put it on Happy's head. Happy was trying to put his head into the halter for the client as he knew what he was trying to do. Regular handling reduces confusion and stress for the horses to try to interpret what the client is wanting of them. Finally, I believe it also adds to a sense of safety for the client, horse and facilitator when working together, using a common language both verbal and non-verbal.

Hoofprints for therapy horse and pony

Here are my hoofprints of expectations of what my therapy horses can and cannot do. I would like my horses to be easy to approach, calm, comfortable working at liberty, soft to lead, and easy to draw and yield to pressure. It would be ideal to have them respect the space of the client. This is where yielding to pressure and cues to back up are really important. The therapy horses that I work with are curious and will step into a client's space, and it is good practice to have the client understand how they can move the horse outside of their space should they wish.

Activities for asking the horse to move outside of one's personal space can also be a good way for clients to learn to set physical boundaries and start noticing their 'space bubble' and feelings of safety and comfort. It can be empowering for the client to set boundaries (moving feet) in the hierarchy of the horse's relationship with the client.

Horses that move or yield from pressure by way of a gentle touch on their hip or shoulder are lovely to work with, especially if you are required to support the client and need to ask the horse to move out of the way. Sometimes, when setting up obstacle courses, the horses walk into the middle of it as a matter of curiosity, so we can ask them to move outside of the obstacle until they are invited in. It all depends on the intervention, but knowing the horses respond to gentle cues is helpful.

As mentioned, horses are social, they read body language, and familiarity means I am part of their herd and I am aware of their character, which assists in understanding their strengths and suitability for various activities. It helps the sessions flow if I have a thorough understanding of every horse's strengths and character.

I have expectations that I can pick up the horse's hooves; this also enables me to work out how they are feeling. Picking up a horse's hooves is a trust exercise. When a horse gives you their hooves, they give you their life because movement is their survival.

I want a horse that can cope with a halter being put on the wrong way, and maybe after a few attempts, so not being head-shy is important. The therapy horse has the right to look after his head and can express it, so I do not 'make' the horse tolerate things they are not feeling comfortable with. They are free to move their heads and walk away if they need to.

I like to be able to brush a therapy horse tied up or not. I would like to tie up one of the horses, without issue, so we can work with another horse. I have the expectation that the horse will be able to tolerate being tied up with little fuss for ten minutes or so. I will provide a bag of hay for them to eat or have grass in reach for them.

As the training of my horses and ponies has progressed, the horses take directions from my hand movements, which has been helpful. For example, the client can walk with the lead rope in a 'smile', like 'holding a pizza', and stop the horse by blowing out air. This reduces the impact of the horse being dragged around by the head and gives the client a gentle focus on leading and on the outbreath, which has a secondary gain of settling the nervous system. In cases where the therapy horse does not want to be led and in order to avoid doing harm, we have taught the horses to follow the client's finger (hand signals) to specific places. I help the client to learn how to do this.

As mentioned, I work with a herd as a resource. The horses and ponies are known to each other and the dynamic is established. I would never bring a new herd member into a session without having them live with their herd until their dynamics are established and I have observed the herd in various mock therapy sessions to see how they will behave. I also want to know their history, age, temperament, and previous training.

A therapy horse or pony should be somewhat predictable and well known to the handler as that relationship and knowledge of the horse or pony will support the observation of their behaviour in session. Regular interactions with the horses by various people, my family and friends, have been important to see not only how the horses react and cope, but also to improve their sense of safety with people not known to them. I have my children ride their bicycles past the horse fence and they throw balls, hoops, and other things around. I work to desensitise by teaching horses they are safe and can tolerate hoops, barrels, pool noodles, cones, tyres being rolled around, mounting blocks (for little children to stand on to brush), flowers, tinsel, fairy wings, and other random dress ups.

The horse trainers I employed were to help me learn the techniques and strategies to work with the horses and get me to a standard of horse handling that was safe in therapy. In regard to horse trainers in Australia at the time of writing this, anyone can call themselves a horse trainer, it is not a regulated industry. I specifically chose people who utilise a relaxation, horse-focused and holistic approach to training and have really enjoyed the journey.

This is a table developed as a guide to assess horse and ponies, focus skills and training for both myself and the horses. It has been adapted over the time to include more skills.

Beginning Therapy horse and pony Re-training 2016	Happy	Trigger	Bob
Who are the horses or ponies? What do I know about them? What do I know about their previous experiences/ training? What do I know about their previous ownership?	Age: 23 years old. Hx: Previously dressage, riding pony, experienced with events and travelling, desensitised to lots of things. A few owners, one owner who would lease Happy out to teach young riders.	Age: 8 years old. Hx: Previously broken in. Attended two shows. Has not been ridden since he was four. Needs to be desensitised to plastic bags, tyres, bicycles. One owner previously broken in by them.	Age: 2 years old. Hx: Not broken in, needs lots of training. Can bite when scared. Needs support and to work with facilitator not clients until understands role. Needs lots of training. One owner previously. Limited training.
Goals for each horse	Look after Happy into old age and nurture him as a senior. Help make him happy and relaxed.	Ride bareback into the sunset and on walking trails around here. Make sure I am an articulate horseperson so he understands my requests, also I understand how to ask and guide. Make sure I can continue to help with his health and wellbeing and manage any pain with his back.	Work with Bob to make sure he is safe for people to be around. So I am proficient at working with him at liberty and he can come for long walks with Trigger and me.

Approach the horse without him walking or running away? This is so important in a therapy session.	Yes, I can approach Happy.	Yes, I can approach Trigger.	Yes, I can approach Bob.
Can other people approach horses?	Yes	Yes	Yes
Lift up Hooves?	I can lift up all of Happy's hooves.	I can lift up two hooves. The right front and the right back. When I lift up the front left, he stomps and the left back he holds it down but can do it. It is not as bad as it used to be. I just keep working on it.	I can lift up Bob's hooves if someone is holding him. I have trouble with his back left hoof, the one with stifle lock so I am a bit tentative with this one.
Does the horse mind being touched over their body? Are there pain spots or areas they do not like to be touched?	I can touch Happy all over. He does not like his groin touched or around his tail.	I can touch everywhere on his back, and stomach. Does not like face to be touched too quickly as he will lift head fast if taken by surprise.	I can touch everywhere. He does not like his face being touched too much and can try to nibble.
Halter? Can others halter the horse?	I can halter Happy. Others can halter.	I can halter Trigger. Others can halter.	I can halter Bob. Bob needs more practise with others haltering him.
Back up horse using rope attached to halter?	I can back up Happy using a rope.	I can back up Trigger using a rope.	I can back up Bob using a rope.
Back up option with touch?	I can back up Happy using touch on his head and shoulders.	I can back up Trigger touching his head, and chest.	I can back up Bob touching his head and shoulders.
Yield at the head, neck, shoulders, and forequarters?	Yes.	Yes.	Still working on yielding at shoulders and forequarters.

Leading forwards, around in circles, over obstacles?	I can lead Happy. I need to wait and then walk. No pulling at all.	I can lead Trigger.	Bob walks backwards. Needs more work. Won't go over some obstacles depending on the day.
Safety driving the horse from behind?	I can drive Happy.	I can drive Trigger.	I can drive Bob.
Obstacles Poles Around Over	Happy will go over, around and through obstacles, but need some support with going through. Will try to avoid going over poles.	Trigger can go through, around and over.	Bob will walk and then stop at raised poles. Poles on the ground he will step over. He will go around obstacles.
Drawing the horse towards you?	I can draw Happy – slowly, as he can head toss.	I can draw Trigger.	I can draw Bob.

Guideline 2: Worksafe, legislations and risk management plans

The reality of caring for horses is that it costs money, takes time and is an ongoing investment into these sentient animals. At the time of writing this book, there are a number of legislations and guidelines for inexperienced people working with horses. The legislations have been endorsed by Worksafe and therefore must be taken seriously when providing equine-assisted therapy. Work and health laws vary from state to state in Australia. Ensure you are aware of what legislation your state has in place for your business. Horse Safety Australia has Safe Work Australia's *Guide to managing risks when new and inexperienced persons interact with horses*, which is endorsed in all states but Victoria.

Worksafe Victoria has a number of guidelines for agriculture and working in farm settings. It is worth a read and having some thought about how to incorporate their guidelines into your workplace policy and procedures.

It is better to have some guidelines to follow of this nature to make sure you are providing a safe working environment. SafeWork NSW's Code of Practice in managing risks when new or inexperienced riders or handlers interact with horses in the workplace applies in NSW.

The Australian Horse Industry Council is a key body in Australia for all things horse activity related. If you are not familiar with them please do read through their website and information. They do not have anything specific on therapy horse per se but many of their codes apply to the work you will do with therapy horses, venues and keeping everyone safe. In addition, Horse Safety Australia, is another key body that is a leader in Australia in setting safety standards for the broader horse industry. It provides training and standards for safety and education. These guidelines may change and be updated. It is important you also stay up to date with changes. It is your responsibility.

In terms of risk management plans, a framework for applying principles of best practice that are employed by Work Health and Safety Acts pertaining to your venue is suitable for equine activities, and your specific workplace. Having a risk management plan that focuses on the physical and emotional safety of children, and people who are participating is essential.

Harnessing Wellness is a child-safe organisation in line with the Department of Human and Health safety guidelines. All staff have valid Working with Children Checks and first aid certification. We have adopted clear recruitment procedures for staff; for example, referee checks and qualification checks. We also provide staff with information or training around the venue, environments and provide support in their roles. I choose not to have volunteers unless they are a psychology student and their placement is going towards registration. Who you hire to work with you is your choice.

There are other codes under the state and federal governments in Australia that offer guidelines for good care and horse husbandry for equines. For example, under Animal Welfare Victoria there is the Prevention of Cruelty to Animals (POCTA) Act, Prevention of Cruelty to Animals Regulations 2019, and there is the Welfare of Horses (Revision 1). This code is used to prosecute people for mistreating and neglecting horses. There are other codes of practice for other species of animals too. In Australia, The Prevention of Cruelty to Animals Act 2019, 'Code of Practice for the Welfare of Horses (Revision 1)' was prepared in consultation with expertise in equine management, welfare and veterinary science. Under this code, the minimum standards of conduct to avoid cruelty to horses are set. In addition to the Five Domains of Wellbeing gives a guide to think about the holistic wellbeing of equines in general and those working in therapy with people.[18]

This is general information, so please do more research in finding out the welfare guidelines of your area and country and legislations relevant to you.

Guideline 3: Equine health

My horses and ponies do not participate in sessions if they are unwell. I have had Trigger with colic before a session. Bob

---

18. Mellor, DJ. (2017), 'Operational Details of the Five Domains Model and Its Key Applications to the Assessment and Management of Animal Welfare.' *Animals* (Basel). 2017 Aug; 7(8): 60. DOI: 10.3390/ani7080060 PMID: 28792485

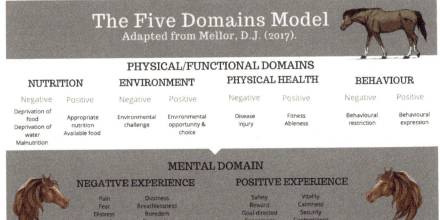

The Five Domains Model
Adapted from Mellor, D.J. (2017).

PHYSICAL/FUNCTIONAL DOMAINS

NUTRITION		ENVIRONMENT		PHYSICAL HEALTH		BEHAVIOUR	
Negative	Positive	Negative	Positive	Negative	Positive	Negative	Positive
Deprivation of food	Appropriate nutrition	Environmental challenge	Environmental opportunity & choice	Disease Injury	Fitness Ableness	Behavioural restriction	Behavioural expression
Deprivation of water	Available food						
Malnutrition							

MENTAL DOMAIN

NEGATIVE EXPERIENCE		POSITIVE EXPERIENCE	
Pain	Dizziness	Safety	Vitality
Fear	Breathlessness	Reward	Calmness
Distress	Boredom	Goal-directed	Security
Discomfort	Frustration	Enagement	Contentment
Disability	Anger	Playfullness	Sociability
Weakness		Curiosity	Companionship

WELFARE STATUS

has developed laminitis overnight and Happy has developed diarrhoea. Trigger has had peritonitis and treatment that lasted three months; he did not participate in sessions but was in view of the clients as Bob and Happy were in sessions. I let people know that he was not able to engage as he was feeling unwell. Most people had questions but were not overly upset about it.

At the time of writing this book, Trigger developed stringhalt, a clinical condition in horses that is characterised by extreme exaggerated flexion of the hindlimbs. Unfortunately, Trigger grazed flatweed following a dry summer and the weed was toxic. He has been removed from the pasture.

All horses should have appropriate veterinary care, their feet trimmed, and be wormed regularly. A rotational worming dosing of horses with different classes of worming active ingredients is often recommended for controlling worms.

The way you look after your horses reflects in their wellbeing too.

The more the horses and ponies social, emotional, and physical needs are met, the happier they are and the more they can function when they are working with myself and clients. The Five Domains Model and the Code of Welfare for Horses (picture on the left) are supportive of assessing equines holistically, and a good guide to use to make sure the wellbeing of each area is addressed. They need: physical space to run, walk and graze; mental stimulation and emotional support from other herd members; shelter for protection; access to fresh nutritional food and water and many other things outlined in the matrix of the five domains.

According to the Code of Practice for the Welfare of Horses and The Five Domains, all horses should have some access to pasture and hay, water, mineral and salt blocks. They should have shelter, trees and areas to walk, run, roll and play. My belief is that the horse or pony should always have a choice to participate in sessions and I have let horses out of sessions if they clearly do not want to be there. This goes back to understand that the equine is a sentient being and you can observe them using heterospecific referential communication.

There is both a human first aid kit and an equine first aid kit at the venue I am working at. If I have staff working with me, I let them know where the kit is for the equines and for the humans. I have the human kit located in my office and the equine first aid kit is easily accessible from the outdoor working area. I do check my horses before we go into sessions, to make sure they are physically and mentally well. You should become familiar with signs and behaviours of different health issues with horses.

Since working with horses, I have learnt about equine warts, eye infections, grass seeds in the eye, laminitis, colic, peritonitis, Cushing's disease, teeth issues, worming, the various types of worms and the impacts they have on the horses, and more recently stringhalt. Learn as much as you can about horses and their health; it will serve you and your therapy horse well. The other thing I have learnt is to have a good, trusted veterinarian, horse vet dentist, spinal vet, barehoof farrier and horse trainer. This team of people are known to each other and support each other's work, and therefore are supportive of my therapy horses' wellbeing and development.

I have listed a first aid kit checklist as an example below. Please make up your own kit and have it available. The area you work from may require other items, so make up your first aid kit accordingly.

Equine First Aid Kit	Checked
Basic First Aid notes – See Horse Vitals Checklist below.	
Vets phone number	
Wire cutters	
Scissors	
Head torch/large touch	
Adhesive tape, Adhesive strips and patches (sterile Band-Aids)	
Bio-disposal bags and gloves	
Hoof picks	
Sterile covering for serious wounds	
Cotton wool and gauze, sterile; small, medium and large wound dressings	
Old rags	
Gaffer tape – electrical tape	
Poultice for abscesses	
Equine thermometer	
Stethoscope, etc.	
* When talking to vet over phone (also learn how to take your horses pulse on their hoof – it is so helpful – speak to you vet about this.	
10 ml and 20 ml syringes.	
Note pad and pen – tracking horses vital signs.	
In case of bushfires or emergency evacuations, I have key tags with each horse and ponies name on them and my phone number. I keep these in the first aid kit too.	

The veterinarian may ask you to check the horses heart rate and temperature. It is important you have these written down and after my experiences with Trigger getting sick, I take these first then call the vet. Speak to your vet about their preferred process and get them to help you work out a baseline of your horse's heartrate and temperature as different breeds of equine may vary from the below.

General horse vital check list. These may vary from horse to horse; these are general. Please check your own horse or learn from your vet.

Horse temperature: Normal 37–38°C

Pulse: At rest 28–44 beats per minute. 32 Normal (One way to do this is to count for 15 seconds and multiply by four.)

Respiration (Breathing): At rest is 8–15 breaths per minute.

Gut sounds: Left side constant gurgling. Right side every 30+ seconds comes a gurgling sound.

Dehydration: Pinch test at neck, skin should flatten in 1 second.

Capillary refill time (CRT): Press gums for 2 seconds should take 1–2 seconds to return to pink.

Mucous membrane: If gums are very pale, bright red, greyish blue or bright yellow, the call the vet. Gums should feel slippery and viscous. If sticky, this could indicate impaction. I just call the vet anyway and do not mess around with these things if you suspect colic.

Guideline 4: Venue choice is important

Since 2010, I have run equine-assisted therapy sessions for individuals and groups at equestrian centres, private farms and pony clubs. Ensuring privacy is an issue. Public areas of equestrian centres and pony clubs were challenging with the public watching. Some came over to ask what we were doing. Managing the public watching, walking their horses past the sessions, horses running over to greet other horses, people standing on the side of the arena watching and asking questions of the participants or even riding their horses into the session, minimised the therapeutic experience, I believe.

Therefore, I choose to work and hire a private farm space that is hidden from public view and is accessible by appointment only. It has toilet facilities, shelter and a counselling room. There are various spaces to work from too, depending on the weather.

The counselling room faces the horses.

Signage upon entry of the property/therapy area

Psychology, Counselling and Equine-assisted Psychology.
Please read.

At Harnessing Wellness we work with our horses and ponies
to train and socialise them to interact with people.

Horses by nature are prey, play and flight animals. If they
are frightened, they resort to their instincts to stay safe and
survive. Therefore, their behaviour can be unpredictable and
may result in injury to the participants or spectators.

Participants who attend Harnessing Wellness's equine-assisted
psychology programs must be aware there are risks. Please
read the indemnity forms well to give informed consent. You
will not be able to participate without these signed.

At all times, participants and spectators are to be responsible
for their own self-care, awareness of the environment and
must adhere to staff advice and guidelines.

SAFETY GUIDELINES INCLUDE

No entry into the paddock without a staff member.

- Welcome to Harnessing Wellness. We look forward to working with you and the horses.

- You will be advised to follow safety information and walk slowly and calmly around the horses.

- Please listen to instructions around the horses. This is to keep you, the horses and others safe.

- Anyone deemed substance affected is not permitted to attend or participate in therapy sessions or go near the horses.

- Weather appropriate clothing is to be worn, including hats. Closed-toed shoes such as gumboots or runners are to be worn.

- No feeding horses.

- No food or drinks to be taken past the office and into the equine-assisted therapy session.

- Please ask a staff member if you have questions.

- Please use hand sanitiser before and after the session.

Guideline 5: Develop a fire, flood, and plans to cancel sessions due to weather

Fire plans are essential. Also have one for the property and horses if it floods or snows in your area, etc. I will talk more about fire danger days as we have many of them here. I have had to choose to continue or discontinue working with clients and the horses on fire danger days. Given my training in critical incidents, being prepared and planning ahead are in my thoughts so I generally cancel and reschedule sessions. The thought of working and checking the Victorian Emergency App to see if there is a fire approaching is not working within my scope of duty of care to my clients, my horses and myself and family. Check your local Country Fire Authority (CFA) for more information about planning a fire plan for your place of work.

I have key tags with the horses' names and phone number on it and they can be attached and braided to the horse's mane or tail in an emergency. I remove all halters and fly veils as they can melt in extreme heat or get caught on trees, fences or gates and cause injury. Basically, be prepared.

I have cancelled sessions on fire danger days and clients have been understanding of this decision. Safety overrides everything. In other weather conditions I have also assessed and cancelled, in particular when there was torrential rain and bad wind. I usually have indoor activities planned if going outdoors is going to be challenging such as the rain, wind or mud. I make decisions based on client safety and horse safety. I ask questions such as, *Is it muddy? Will they slip? Is it safe?*

Guideline 6: Infectious disease controls

The world locked down to reduce the spread of COVID-19. In March 2020, we went onto stage 3 lockdown in Victoria, Australia. During this time, we emailed all of our clients that we were moving to telehealth options and I ceased doing equine-assisted therapy for about a year.

I did an online course for infectious disease control. We developed a policy for our clinic room, equine-assisted psychology and the venue. It basically stated that we were committed to reducing the risks of exposure of illness to our staff, clients and horses while attending appointments with us. You will have to develop your own procedures suited to your local area, and get Government Department advice about the issue at hand. We stopped doing equine-assisted therapy as we could not socially distance (1.5 metres) while with the horses.

We followed the Department of Human and Health guidelines around infectious control if some people came into the office for face-to-face session, but when we went into stage 4 lockdown no one attended psychology in person.

This was updated as new guidelines were given and put in the equine therapy and counselling office:

- Use hand sanitiser as you enter the office.

- Please remove your shoes as the virus lasts on surfaces for up to 72 hours.

- Wash hands for a minimum 20 seconds regularly.

- Always cough into your elbow and throw away used tissues.

- Stay home if you are unwell and have symptoms such as coughing, cold, fever, runny nose, sore throat, and body aches.

We emailed our clients this statement at the start of March 2020. 'If you participate in equine-assisted psychology sessions, we can offer online counselling in the paddock with the horses but not face-to-face as social distancing would be difficult to maintain with the horses.' Always check the government infectious control advice.

People who were involved with equine therapy were very understanding. Some chose to see the horses online, while others chose to wait to return to sessions.

As it is your business you are able to choose your level of safety. Minimising risk to yourself, horses and clients will enable your business to develop a good reputation, and having a plan in how you operate during uncertain times will enable flexibility in your services. Staying safe to look after yourself, clients and your horses is most important.

Step Eight

The Clinical Room and Equine Facilities

A horse gallops with his lungs, perseveres
with his heart, and wins with his character.

– Federico Tesio

Following on from the last chapter, I am going to elaborate on the work location. As mentioned, the venue is very important. It is in the office, the safe space, the area in which the therapy occurs. It is where the horses, humans and psychologists need to feel safe, comfortable and able to function as 'naturally' as possible.

We chose a place that was a blank canvas. I searched for five years for a 'perfect venue'. I had had experience working in equestrian centres, riding schools, pony clubs and all were okay for the time, but not ideal and I was less than happy with the distractions. Issues working in those venues included people coming and going with their horses (even though I had hired the space), parents wanting to be involved and watching the client, which could potentially become an issue for the client not feeling free to express themselves without feeling judged.

I have found it important that the space to work from was not a formal equestrian setting. I believe by removing it from formal venues places, equine-assisted psychology changes the expectations of it being similar to a horse-riding lesson. It is an adjunct therapy, not a process of mastering the horse.

The venue that we constructed was not like others I had worked at. The arena was halfway down a hill, so exercise was involved when walking to and from the arena. The arena was three-quarters the size of a normal arena. It had a big horse shelter at one end. A sail cloth was erected initially as Trigger would not allow the others in the shelter during summer, and the arena was part of a track system so horses could come and go and pass through it. There were no surprises for the horses when it came to therapy sessions as they were able to access the arena and shelter as part of their daily track walking. They were not floated to and from the venue, therefore they were at their home and working in it.

The purpose of this was that the horses were not activated into flight before equine-assisted psychology sessions. They were calm and could focus on the client when they attended. It also facilitates an environment in which they feel at home and act as they would normally during their day, which I believe reduces stress and unnecessary distractions. Horses and ponies used to being floated regularly without stress and used to moving through other environments, I imagine, would cope, but that would be up to the facilitator to decide because they understand their horses and have trained them to travel without stress.

I do a lot of the training with the horses in the venue to work out how they will act and respond to different stimuli, such as barrels and tyres rolling around, as well as chairs, cones and other objects used as obstacles. They are familiar with the weather, winds, sun, rain, hail and therefore it reduces surprises, like scary plastic bags. When I work with horses at the venue, they have already experienced mock practise activities and been around the equipment, and the repetition and familiarity reduce their stress and increase their knowledge of what may be asked of them by the client.

Horses are routine animals. Routine and predictability means safety, therefore bringing new people into the herd and their environment means the herd is stable in their environment and more able to hold space and interact with the clients authentically and without heightened energy. I am not saying that the horse's energy and focus is not heightened when new people come into the sessions, I am saying that by being in a familiar environment I aim to reduce additional nervous system activation and it also enables me to identify any hazards and potential risks.

The venue has a clinic room on site with a toilet, and there is a beautiful view. The venue also allows work with the horses near the clinic room, another area they are familiar with. In wet weather, I bring the ponies and horses up near the clinic room and can work there in relative comfort from the rain, and there is a shelter to groom the ponies under cover. I understand that everyone's situation will be different, therefore this information is a guide about what I have done and the reasons behind it. I can also use the venue to see clients who would like face-to-face psychological counselling and many have commented on the view.

The physical practice – confidential, private and safe working environment

The arena

I work from an outdoor arena. It offers the experience of being outdoors and in the elements of the weather. I work in all sorts of weather, and it becomes a discussion in addition to the horses. Within reason, being a little cold or a little hot or uncomfortable in our environment can build resilience and also offers conversations about self-care. The other reason I like an outdoor arena is that it offers opportunities to feeding, learn hoof care and the horses are in an environment where they can graze when there is grass. There is a water trough for access to water at all times, so the horses' needs are being met as much as possible during the session.

Equipment in sessions

I use a 12-foot lead rope and rope halter and I teach the clients how to use it. They can be harder to put on than the halters with metal buckles, but it teaches clients patience and the ability to be in close proximity to the horse. I do have a variety of halters for different abilities.

The use of a halter and lead rope is a form of communication with the horse. I teach the client not to pull on the halter or the lead rope but to use it as a form of feel and communication between themselves and the horses head. This has been a lovely lesson in gentle touch, patience and can evoke conversations around safe touch, communication strategies and setting boundaries.

Due to the majority of clients being inexperienced horse people, and depending on the reason for attending counselling, some clients are not able to empathise with the horse being a thinking, feeling, sentient being in the initial sessions. There are also people who are too scared to touch the halter and lead rope for fear of hurting the horses. Both of these scenarios offer clinical information and can help formulate the treatment plan.

Each horse and pony have their own colour lead rope and halter. Trigger is blue, Happy is purple, and Bob and Bailey are red and white but they can share. The reason to use a long rope is to allow the clients to have some distance away from the horse; they do not lead under the neck and are off the horse, as in the horse is off and away from the client. The clients get to know the colours, which helps create familiarity and confidence in the process of interacting with these horses. I also have an array of dress up items for fun activities such as brushes, hair ties, bows, clips, feather boas, and themed items for holidays such as tinsel for around Christmas time.

In terms of items for making and using in activities, I have small and large cones, hula hoops, poles, tyres, barrels, poles cut into quarters, thick long ropes, hoses, white boards to draw on, an A-frame with a blank sign to write on, halters, balls, tennis balls, soccer balls, chairs, pool noodles, and rocks for building and placing (not throwing). Offering any piece of equipment to a client is a choice point around safety for themselves, you and

the horse. I have signs, flags, horse balls and play mats that can be like a puzzle on the ground. There are horse dress-ups too. You can be as imaginative with equipment as you like.

Plants and grass

I have learnt a lot about pasture and fodder trees. I wanted my horses to have access to low sugar grasses, so for the arena there is bent grass and native grasses sown. The trees that are planted in and around the arena are fodder trees. There are Tagasaste (Lucerne trees), Salt Bush, Acacia trees, Manuka Bush, and Bottle Bush planted near the arena. This is a fascinating area of learning and I encourage you to find out more about what fodder trees and herbs may be beneficial for your horses and what pastures are the most suited depending on where you are, the soil and the weather.

Step Nine

Manage Your Emotions

A good horseperson knows how to
manage his emotions.

– Bruck Brennanan

Be an attuned horse handler

I absolutely believe the quote above by Bruck Brennanan. I think it applies to many things in life. The better skills you have in understanding and managing your emotions, the more you can learn and connect with others and achieve challenging tasks. Understanding your emotions, your ability to regulate how you feel around different horses and ponies and staying present in the moment helps, so you and the horse are able to meet each other emotionally.

When we are present we can make clear intentions and this communication is easier for the horses to understand without the communication getting muddied in your emotional landscape.

A horse is never 'wrong', they live moment to moment and adjust as they are required to in the situation they are in. Depending on the work you do, the horse will look to you as a leading herd member in therapy sessions, and that is where understanding

your horse's psychology and body language is an important aspect of equine-assisted therapy.

During therapy sessions the horses will look towards you for guidance, therefore having a partnership with your horse is important for leading them through any tricky therapy sessions. Sometimes, I think Trigger rolls his eyes at me like 'not this again' when he is being led around and through an obstacle. As mentioned before, horses do not speak human, so understanding and being patient with your horse and teaching others to do so in therapy sessions, is supportive of the horse being a keen participant.

Being clear in asking your horse what to do is important, as horses cannot read between the lines. Managing your energy

around horses is important. To be aware of your level of energy and to regulate the energy before and during equine-therapy sessions are equally as important to encouraging safety. If you arrive late for a session, and the client is waiting, you both walk to the area for the therapy session. If you are a bit flustered, not only will the client pick up on it but the horses will too. It is paramount to slow down, breath and bring yourself into the moment before you begin a therapy session. It is best practice to be a safe dependable horse person who can regulate emotions for the therapy horse. It eliminates additional unknown factors for your therapy horse especially if they are trying to read your body language and understand your intention.

It is important as a therapist who works with horses, to be aware not only of your horses' strengths and areas for growth but also your own. Accept your areas for doing further work, for within that lies your power and connection with your horse, as you will allow yourself to be guided by the horse as to what is needed in terms of communication. You will not be able to offer more to your clients than your own knowledge of horse-handling competencies.

A horse's commitment is simple and unconditional, and that serves us well if we too do not objectify them for our own interest. Whether through training or other activities, if we use fear to get horses to do what we want, we will neither gain trust nor respect of the horse and it will serve as a barrier to the relationship with the horse.

Fear can influence yourself and a client. A horse's fear of something can evoke fear in humans and vice versa. The same thing is true if you are not able to manage your emotions with a horse. Similarly, behaving aggressively can evoke aggression in the human and the other way around too. Studies have shown that horses do not appear to understand the emotions of anger, frustration, and impatience, and these emotions can evoke fear in them. Therefore, knowing how to manage your emotions is part of being and working with horses.

Step Ten

Therapy Equine Health and Clients

A great horse will change your life. The truly
special ones define it.

– Unknown

My Trigger, big heart, lots of hugs

On 16 March 2016, Trigger developed acute colic and, over the following days, peritonitis. I was filling up the water baths in the arena when he laid down in front of me, which I thought was quite strange. He got up and walked, then followed me across the arena when I noticed he started kicking the wall of the arena, stomping and kicking. Panic flooded me and I thought, *Oh no, this is colic, looks like … please don't be colic.* From what I had heard from people talking about horses having colic, it was not a good scenario unfolding. Actually, most of my worst fears of my horses getting ill have happened.

I walked up to my office, and Trigger followed me up the hill from the arena, laying down outside the office window in the pasture. I went inside to call the veterinarian; I walked towards the window to see Trigger. He was sweating, laying down. He was not moving. I was shaking and I started to cry, my default reaction when overwhelmed.

The vet was able to come within 25 minutes. When the vet arrived, he looked shocked at what he saw. I had tears streaming down my face and one of the neighbours had come past and luckily stopped in to help. I will always be indebted to this neighbour; he was calm and supported the process brilliantly. Had it not been for his steady presence, I think I would have been worse. The three of us worked to get Trigger (650 kg) to his feet. He was sedated and a tube was put down his throat – it all happened very quickly. The vet then said that we wait and see which end something comes out of and that will give us an indication of what was going on. Then I was told to watch Trigger for the next few hours, and that he would come back at 6 pm.

Depending on Trigger's presentation at 6pm I was to report back to him by 10pm. Hence my knowledge of horse vitals, and my extensive first aid kit. He also said that if things did not improve he knew a guy with an excavator. I had tears running down my face, but I knew I had to just go with the process. I had also sent a message to my clients to cancel their appointments for the afternoon. I explained it was a personal matter and would need to reschedule them.

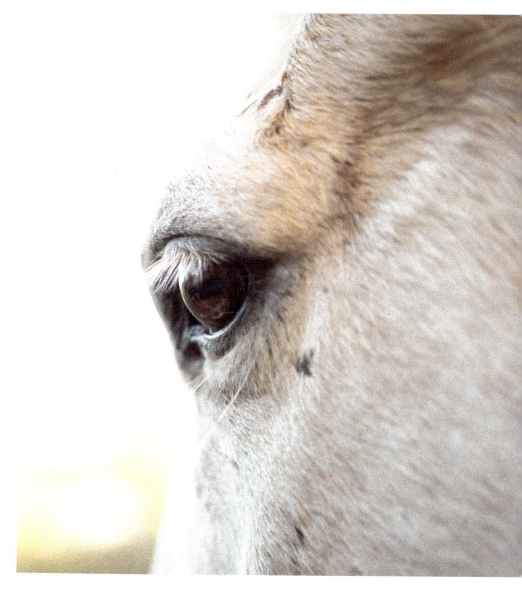

At 6pm the vet returned. We walked Trigger to the arena under shelter, where it was covered and I rugged him. Water was also easy to access. The vet offered options, one was to take Trigger to the equine hospital, but I was concerned he may die of stress. I decided to stay with him and bring the herd closer to him for support and comfort. Trigger did not move, as the vet sedated him again to relax him. I stayed in the arena with Trigger that night, it was a little scary with noises of nocturnal animals scurrying around, and I am not that brave. By 10pm that night, Trigger had done a poo, it was the most excited I had been to see horse poo.

I took photos and sent them to the vet and friends and family. The poo meant it was not a twisted bowel among other things. The vet called as he wanted all of the vital signs, temperature, heart rate, and gum test. I had a notebook and started writing Trigger's observation down hourly.

The choices I made for Trigger over this period of time were my choices. They needed to be made based on my knowledge of Trigger, his personality, my support and finances (yes, sometimes the reality is these do come into question). They may not be what other people would do, but they were what I thought was best for Trigger at the time.

Later in the evening, my husband came to join me, he sat and rubbed Trigger's tummy. My parents were looking after our children. As the sun came up, the horses that lived next door were all standing by the fence and stayed there for the next few days while Trigger was really unwell. A kookaburra also stayed on the fence and perched in a nearby tree for a couple of weeks.

The vet came first thing in the morning. I had been noting down Trigger's heart rate and temperature every hour and did so for the next two weeks, it was around-the-clock care. The vet was surprised Trigger lived. The story goes on.... Trigger had an allergic reaction to the antibiotics he was on, and developed oedema in his legs and sheath area. We changed the antibiotics. It took about six weeks for Trigger to be walking properly again and settled. The vet said to this day he still cannot believe that he was alive. In my mind, I kept focusing on wellbeing and care.

While I went to work and began to see some clients, I explained that Trigger was unwell and integrated this into the session, if it was relevant, and discussed sickness, rest and self-care. Trigger was not in the equine-assisted therapy sessions, he was in the paddock next to the arena while the other horses and ponies were working. The lessons that I learnt from Trigger getting sick were how important it is to understand horse vital signs; to become comfortable enough to put a thermometer in the rectum to test temperature, how to take the heart rate by the hoof and to learn how to check the gums to see if there is white or red around the outside of the teeth. I had to learn to listen to gut sounds, assess if he was dehydrated and administer medicine orally and as an injection. I had to learn confidence to calm Trigger down and mostly calm myself first.

A massive help in this experience, and which helped Trigger, was that I could handle and touch Trigger all over his body. He was not worried or startled, he was comfortable to be touched and did not stress. Trigger being sick was very stressful, but having a supportive vet team and other professionals made it a smoother experience. These included a barefoot farrier, a horse vet dentist and spinal vet. These people are some of the most beautiful people who love and treat horses holistically. They are also people who treat my herd well. When Trigger was feeling better, he walked towards the arena during a client's session and I allowed him into the session without any leading or asking to do any more than eating.

Four years later, Trigger, registered name Kanukadale Golden Ticket, developed Stringhalt and bilateral peripheral atrophy in both hind legs. I worked hard feeding him all of the different vitamins, fresh food, and arranging regular acupuncture. Unfortunately, on Thursday, 21 January 2021, Trigger was laid to rest after a year of battling Stringhalt symptoms. He did make some recovery in August 2020, but the nerve damage in his hind legs was too much. The week prior was one of the hardest decisions I have had to make; his ability to walk became compromised. It was a heartbreaking process to watch.

We were in lockdown due to COVID-19, so I had not done equine therapy for the most part of the year, while he was unwell. I spent more time with him and value that gratefully. His passing was a peaceful one, but very sad.

I decided not to put information on social media at the time, as he had been with many of the clients that follow Harnessing Wellness. It is a choice point how you support the grief and loss process of a therapy animal. If you put up their passing on social media- depending on the client- you may not be able to contain their grief. I did tell clients prior to his passing that he was not well. Many of them hugged him. And those that knew he had passed away sent flowers, messages of love and thanks and gratitude for being with him. Bob, Bailey and Happy had time to say goodbye too. Bob called and called for Trigger for a few days and that was heartbreaking too. As Trigger was buried, swallow birds began to fly around and Bob and I stood together watching.

Trigger is buried on the property we work at and I visit his resting place regularly. The grief was very real, very physical and emotionally painful. I was lucky enough to be able to choose the vet, a compassionate woman who Trigger knew and who knew and treated other ponies who worked at Harnessing wellness. Trigger worked in therapy with over 400 people over five years. I will be forever grateful for knowing him.

Step Eleven

Case Examples

If you take time to observe children, their behaviour will communicate their needs. Horses are the same, the more you observe them, the clearer it is what they are wishing for.

– Anon

Permission has been given and the case studies have been changed to protect privacy and confidentiality. Any photos in here are used with written permission for educational purposes. Strict copyrights apply. The information here is a guide for what happened in each individual case study and may not be used as a formal treatment plan for other related cases.

When clients arrive at Harnessing Wellness, they are not to be substance affected at the time of interacting with the horses for safety reasons, one of which is a compromised nervous system and inhibited reflexes.

Case study 1:
Safety first for a group of clients with social anxiety

Group: Four adolescent people

Within any group setting to begin the forming of the group, we work to set out parameters of how people can feel safe in the group, physically and emotionally. Safety in equine-assisted therapy, as in general therapy, is important to build rapport. Without safety first, rapport will not be able to be built. In this first case study, it was a group of young people who had expressed 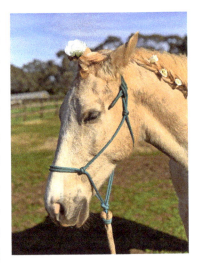 that they felt unsafe and together made a safe space. Before this happened, some adolescents were reluctant to participate in the group. Once their basic need for safety and feeling safe were met, then they were able to engage.

The guidelines were discussed and basically 'what happens, in the paddock stays in the paddock'.

- Trust.

- Be kind.

- Teamwork.

- Respect – everyone has something valuable to contribute.

- No phones.

- You are able to keep yourself safe emotionally and physically, as this contributes to the safety of the group.

Many of the participants reported feeling unsafe, even those who had had horse experience. Strategies for addressing trauma and behaviour would be most successful when they are applied purposefully across a setting in which young people play and learn. Safety can mean different things to different people: feeling safe emotionally, physically and cognitively. The group  collectively decided that putting barrels and cones around them and not letting the horses into the group was the first step to safety. The group then decided to introduce each other to one horse at a time. The facilitator was asked by a group member if they could halter and move the other horses away from the group area. Each group member then met each horse one by one. The session and group were established around safety, coping strategies and keeping others safe.

Case study 2:
The importance of taking time and not rushing processes

This case study is about being able to take the time that a client needs to take. This brief case example is of a young person in an equine-assisted therapy session with significant anxiety – they had been the victim of bullying and assault at school. They would not talk much but spent a lot of the session brushing Happy. After about twenty minutes they would begin to talk and reflect on their week. It would take them time to regulate and be able to find their voice.

Being with the horses allowed this person to take their time to settle, orientate, rest, enjoy the interaction with the horses, and then speak when they were ready. Sometimes, therapy takes time. This was a good reminder to pace the session according to the client's pace with the horses, and how organic learning and change can occur. To measure this change, psychometric testing pre and post and clinical assessment, is always a suitable way to develop and review treatment plans.

Case study 3:
Learning to lead

This client was referred for anxiety management and coping strategies following living in a complex family situation. The client had been learning non-verbal horse behaviour, and in subsequent sessions, learned to touch the horse all over and learned to safe touch with the horse giving permission. In one particular session, the client was learning to walk the horse on lead. The capacity of traumatised young people to learn can be compromised. Do not underestimate the skills and emotional processing involved in leading a horse. This client had to focus, hold the rope with a smile (slack), walk with their eyes up and looking at the direction of where they are going, all the while having the sense of the horse or pony following or not following them. Their neurobiology was stressed and their emotional state was in flux. Working to build confidence in leading a horse or pony for some people can be hard and take time. In this session, the young person worried about the halter hurting the horse, and the pain caused by pulling on the head of the horse. They did not want to do harm to the horse. New experiences and new information may carry with them elements of threat and uncertainty. It took a session of the client playing with the halter on the horse and using different pressure to become comfortable with their own rules about safe-leading of the horse. The client had the power in this situation to be able to work though their own ideas about safe soft touch.

Being with horses does not demand perfection or make comparisons. Relating to horses encourages the development of skills and values that promote emotional health; for example, patience, fairness, commitment, emotional congruency, relaxation and good breathing, clear communication, care and slowing down, firmness and determination, and good and consistent boundaries. Encouragement boosted the client to accept and value themselves and their achievements.

Case study 4:
Unconditional love at the end of life

Horses are social animals. They have a strong need to be with others. This case study is of a person at the end of their life due to illness and coming to terms with the reality of dying. The feeling of 'love and connection' is one of the highest human needs; this is also true for horses, whether this be the love and connection of a herd or a companion.

This session was around the need to be in the moment, feel love in the moment and not be judged or pitied. This client sat on a chair and the three horses walked towards them. They stood up to be with the horses, touching two with outstretched arms. The horses did not move, and the client then leaned into and cried into the mane of one of the ponies. No one moved. This client sobbed and sobbed. The client expressed out-loud how they knew there was nothing more to do but live their last few months, they expressed regrets and what they were grateful for. No one moved. When the client stopped sobbing, Happy, the medium-sized pony, put his head on the client's shoulder. The client interpreted it as an unconditional hug.

*We will never have to tell our horse that we
are sad, happy, confident, angry, or relaxed.
He already knows – long before we do.*

– Marjike de Jong

Step Twelve

Harnessing Wellness

*One who believes that he has mastered the
art of horsemanship has not yet begun to
understand the horse.*

– Unknown

Horses teach us about honesty and authenticity because they know no other way of being. They teach us to respect us about collaboration over dominance. And they teach us to respect and honour the unknown rather than to fear it and try to destroy it.

~ Unknown ~

HARNESSING WELLNESS

My learning of working with horses in therapy began when I attended an equine-assisted therapy training on the weekend of the Black Saturday Bushfires in Victoria, Australia. My reason for doing the training was purely out of personal interest. I never thought it would give me a purpose.

My day job was working in the local shire as a youth mental health worker, and following that weekend in February 2009, I was part of a bushfire support recovery team. While working in a recovery centre in the Yarra Ranges in 2009, I met Dr Rob Gordon, who is a psychologist and someone who had worked with people recovering from various natural disasters. I began to read his literature. I also attended online lectures at 3 am Melbourne time by Dr Janina Fisher, an American psychotherapist, on sensory-motor psychotherapy, learning how the body remembers trauma and tries to process the experience. The work these people were doing assisted in providing frameworks and a longer term view of how the equine-assisted programs/therapy could assist the bushfire-affected community. I also had connections with community support workers to debrief and find out what the community needed at that time, as community recovery needed change.

The long-term consequences on mental health after experiencing a natural disaster can be ongoing, possibly for years. In my own experience, following the earthquake in Japan, and as learned from others, sometimes you do not even recognise the symptoms. The issues may be due to reduced physical and psychological health as a consequence of the event itself. Furthermore, there may a change in interpersonal relationships and social dynamics during the recovery phase. Some people may not access mental health services, but rather engage in informal networks of friends, and family. However those part of the informal networks may already feel overwhelmed and stressed by the situation and or event.

In 2009, the initial request from the Bushfire Recovery Unit was to develop a support program for families that prefer alternative outdoor therapy, not traditional counselling. The program was to support people to process emotions, reconnect with their communities and process their experience of grief and loss. I did not have horses at the time, so I hired them and worked with a mental health professional, to help deliver the programs.

From 2010 to 2014, I facilitated the equine-assisted therapy trauma recovery groups. Running the groups gave me insight into areas of learning and growth around incorporating horses in natural disaster recovery.

Some objectives of the recovery program were to:

- create a psychologically safe space for participants to process their individual experiences, including grief, loss, pain, distress, trauma and feelings of anxiety.
- provide an environment for individuals to become aware of their strengths, and to develop resilience and new coping strategies.
- provide psycho-education on the way the body reacts to trauma, and working in a relationship with the horse to strengthen emotional regulation and explore new coping strategies.
- create an environment for individuals to develop an awareness of triggers and build on strengths and self-resources.
- provide experiential activities with horses to develop problem solving, creativity and skills in recognising strengths.
- design the program activities with the focus for individuals to build resilience to stress and to develop psychosocial resources such as coping efforts, self-efficacy, mastery, perceived control, self-esteem, hope and optimism.

The above factors have been found to protect those who have been affected by a natural disaster. Protection afforded by social resources included social support and perceived social support.[19]

Therapeutic activities with the horses is the process. The horse is not the focus, but present to assist and promote reflection and analysis through the client's interpretation of the horse's behaviour and social interaction.

Horses involved themselves when they wanted to, tipping chairs, taking people's hats off, nudging clients, walking away from or walking toward clients, lying down and enjoying a scratch. The program was a combination of guided activities and other activities were discussed by the group. Horses were great models in self-care and this was often reflected on by the clients. Horses assisted in teaching clients to breathe again. Body and mind focused strategies became important as the symptoms and presentations of clients changed.

The activities provided opportunity for metaphorical learning, reframing while challenging unhelpful behaviours, attitudes, ideas and beliefs about relationships and safety of self. The client's response was fundamental to the clinical team.

It was through the client projecting their thoughts and feelings onto the horses, that their perception of their world unfolded. Therapy sessions conducted outdoors enabled clients to actively engage physically, emotionally and socially with the horses and other group members. The structure of the program was eight weeks, at two hours per session. The use of psychometric

---

19. Norris FH, Baker CK, Murphy AD, Kaniasty K. 'Social support mobilization and deterioration after Mexico's 1999 flood: Effects of context, gender and time.' *American Journal of Community Psychology.* 2005; 36:15–28
Solomon SD, Smith EM, Robins LN, Fischbach RL. 'Social involvement as a mediator of disaster-induced stress.' *Journal of Applied Social Psychology.* 1987;17:1092–1112.

testing provided a common clinical communication with other counsellors, case managers, doctors and service providers to discuss the equine-assisted therapy program, treatment plans and the impact on clients.

Following the completion of four years of offering the equine-assisted therapy program, I continued to learn and offer equine-assisted therapy to groups and individuals. Over the years, I have participated in equine-assisted training with various organisations, each with their own philosophies of horses and theory underpinning their training. It was good to get an idea of how various organisations incorporated horses in therapy. Without it, I would not have been able to develop my practices and ideas, but the hands-on experience taught the most. The horse psychology and behaviour course formed the backbone to my understanding of horses too. Working with horses in groups gave me insight into the type of horses and ponies that were suited to this work, and those horses that enjoyed their interactions with people and those that did not, and they all had to be respected.

I was fortunate to work at various venues and environments and this exposure gave me appreciation for a venue developed with the client's confidentiality in mind. The co-facilitators I have worked with over the years, those who really love what they do, and the knowledge and further studies I have engaged in have been awesome. I believe that this exposure has been informative on how to tie all of the parts together, offering successful therapeutic programs for all involved. I have presented at conferences and guest lectured at universities on many of these things.

I have never been nor will be an equestrian. I have trouble balancing in a saddle, so others may have a different view about what and how horses can be incorporated into therapy, but I firmly believe from my experience on the ground that with horses is where the relationship happens.

Currently, we are out of COVID-19 lockdown and into a new year, still wearing face masks. As I wasn't able to work with the horses in 2020 with people face-to-face, I wrote children's books on mental health and coping, *Happy the Very Sad Pony*, *Trigger the Anxious Horse*, and *All Horses Become the Stars* (on grief and loss). I dare say Happy, Bob and Bailey, the little herd that I have been working with are looking forward to seeing people face to face, and I will continue to work with the grief of losing Trigger. Harnessing wellness and building resilience are two things that I am extremely passionate about for people. If horses support these processes for people with more research, then we can support evidence-based practice and further develop animal-assisted therapies in general. I am also a great believer in animal welfare and respect.

It has been an absolute pleasure incorporating horses into therapy, meeting so many different people and horses and ponies along the way and learning how to apply the different evidence-based therapies. The journey, my hoofprints for setting up an equine-assisted therapy clinic, has been hard work, but I hope this gives you a few tips that will help you. From a welfare perspective if an equine is out of work, they may be able to have a second career and work as an therapy equine. With proper assessment and training, they may enjoy a second career helping people. Like Happy. *Hoofprints for Setting up an Equine-Assisted Therapy Clinic* began with a natural disaster and we are currently in a pandemic. The learning of how I can incorporate horses into therapy for people has had its highs and lows.

Over the years people have asked how I began; many people have expressed to me that they would like to do the same sort of work, so this is my 'being in contribution' to the field and for other professionals. This how-to book was a way to impart my experience and knowledge of horses and their welfare, and how to incorporate them into responsible and ethical therapy for people. Equine assisted therapy is growing as a field of adjunct therapy. Please do your research into the methods, training and education available to make the most ethical decision that is right for you, your horses and future clients. Make sure that you understand your skillset and what you can safety offer your clients and how you can work safely with your horses. Always have safety first for the client and horse's welfare at front of mind, one hoofprint at a time.

Best wishes, Naomi and the herd.